MW00461676

MAGIC WORDS

Also by Jonah Berger

MAGIC WORDS

What to Say to Get Your Way

JONAH BERGER

HARPER
BUSINESS

An Imprint of HarperCollins*Publishers*

HarperCollins books may be purchased for educational, business, or sales promotional use. For information, please email the Special Markets Department at SPsales@harpercollins.com.

FIRST EDITION

Library of Congress Cataloging-in-Publication Data
Names: Berger, Jonah, author.
Title: Magic words : what to say to get your way / Jonah Berger.
Description: First edition. | New York, NY : HarperCollins Publishers, [2023] | Includes bibliographical references and index. | Summary: "A book about how to use words in a way that is most persuasive"—Identifiers: LCCN 2022023797 (print) | LCCN 2022023798 (ebook) | ISBN 9780063204935 (hardcover) | ISBN 9780063204959 (ebook)
Subjects: LCSH: Persuasion (Psychology) | Communication.
Classification: LCC BF637.P4 B37 2023 (print) | LCC BF637.P4 (ebook) | DDC 153.8/52--dc23/eng/20220716
LC record available at https://lccn.loc.gov/2022023797
LC ebook record available at https://lccn.loc.gov/2022023798

23 24 25 26 27 LBC 5 4 3 2 1

To anyone who has ever marveled at the power of words.

Contents

MAGIC WORDS

Introduction

When he was just over a year old, our son, Jasper, started saying the word "please." Or at least trying to. He couldn't pronounce his *L*'s yet, so it ended up sounding more like "peas," but it was close enough for us to get the main thrust of what he was saying.

His use of the word, in itself, wasn't that surprising. After all, by six months old most kids can recognize basic sounds, and around a year they can usually say one to three words.

What was interesting, though, was the way he'd use it.

He'd say something he wanted, like "up," "yo" (yogurt), or "brow ber" (his stuffed brown bear) and then pause to note the result. If he got what he wanted right away, that would be it. He wouldn't say anything else. But if he didn't get what he wanted, or if you seemed to be doing anything other than hustling to get him what he'd asked for, he'd look you straight in the eye, nod his head, and say the word "peas."

As Jasper got older, his vocabulary grew. He started talking about his favorite creatures ("dido!" for dinosaurs), things he wanted to do ("wee" for slides), and counting ("two"). He even added the word "yeah" to follow "peas" to show that he really meant business. As in "yo," "peas," "yeah." Or translated to adult English, "Yes, I'd like yogurt . . . .—I mean it."

But "peas" was special. Because "peas" was the first time he realized that words have power. That they drive action. That if he wanted something and it wasn't coming, adding the word "peas" would make it happen. Or at least make it more likely.

Jasper had discovered his first magic word.

Almost everything we do involves words. We use words to communicate ideas, express ourselves, and connect with loved ones. They're how leaders lead, salespeople sell, and parents parent. They're how teachers teach, policymakers govern, and doctors explain. Even our private thoughts rely on language.

By some estimates, we use around sixteen thousand words a day.[1] We write emails, build presentations, and talk to friends, colleagues, and clients. We draft online dating profiles, chat with neighbors, and touch base with partners to see how their day went.

But while we spend a lot of time using language, we rarely think about the specific language we use. Sure, we might think about the *ideas* we want to communicate, but we think a lot less about the particular *words* we use to communicate them. And why should we? Individual words often seem interchangeable.

Take the third to last sentence you just read. While it used the word "particular" to refer to words, it could have just as easily used the word "individual," "specific," or any number of other synonyms. While getting our point across is obviously important, the particular words used to do so often seem inconsequential. Happenstance turns of phrase, or whatever happened to come to mind.

But it turns out that intuition is wrong. Very wrong.

THE WORD THAT CHANGED THE WORLD

In the 1940s, one word was enough to change the world. Whenever disaster struck, or evildoers threatened to destroy life as we know it, comic book teenager Billy Batson would say SHAZAM! and transform into a superhero with extraordinary strength and speed.

Such magic words have been around forever. From "Abracadabra!" and "Hocus-pocus!" to "Open sesame!" and "Expecto patronum!," magicians, wizards, and heroes of all stripes have used language to conjure up mystical powers. Like enchanting spells, certain words, used strategically, could change, or do, anything. Listeners were powerless to resist them.

Clearly fiction, right? Not quite.

In the late 1970s, researchers from Harvard University approached people using a copy machine in the library at the City University of New York and asked them for a favor.[2]

New York is known for its vibrant culture, tasty food, and diverse melting pot of people. But friendliness? Not so much. New Yorkers are known for talking fast, working hard, and always being in a rush. So getting them to inconvenience themselves to help a stranger would be difficult, to say the least.

The researchers were interested in what drives persuasion. A member of the team would wait at a table in the library for someone to start making copies. When the would-be copier placed material on the machine, the team member would intervene. They would walk over to the innocent bystander, interrupt what that person was doing, and ask to cut in front and use the machine.

The researchers tried different approaches. For some people, they made a direct request: "Excuse me, I have five pages. May I use the Xerox machine?" For others, they added the word "because," as in "Excuse me, I have five pages. May I use the Xerox machine, *because* I'm in a rush?"

The two approaches were almost identical. Both politely said "Excuse me," both asked to use the machine, and both noted the five pages that needed to be copied. The imposition was the same as well. In both cases, the would-be copier had to stop what they're doing, take their material off the copier, and twiddle their thumbs while someone else went ahead of them.

But the two approaches, while similar, had vastly different effects. Adding the word "because" boosted the number of people who let the researcher skip the line by over 50 percent.

A 50 percent increase in persuasion due to just one word is huge. Astronomical even. But to be fair, one could argue that the two approaches differed in more than just one word. After all, the approach that included the word "because" didn't just add that word, it also added a reason for the request (i.e., that the requester was in a rush).

So rather than "because" driving persuasion, maybe people were more likely to say yes because the reason for the request was really good. The requester said they were in a rush, and the innocent bystander wasn't, so maybe they said yes just to be polite or helpful.

But that wasn't it. Because the researchers also tried one more approach. For a third set of people, rather than giving a valid reason, the requester gave a meaningless one: "Excuse me, I have five pages. May I use the xerox machine, because I have to make copies?"

That time the requester's reason didn't add any new information. After all, by asking to use the copier, it was already clear that the requester needed to make copies. So tacking on that one word—"because"—shouldn't have mattered. If giving a valid reason was what boosted persuasion, then saying they needed to use the machine because they needed to make copies shouldn't have helped. In fact, given that the reason was meaningless, it might even reduce persuasion, making people less likely to agree.

But that's not what happened. Rather than decreasing persuasion, including a meaningless reason actually increased it—just as much as the valid reason did. Persuasion wasn't driven by the reason itself. It was driven by the power of the word that came before it: "because."

The Copy Machine study is just one example of the power of magic words. Saying you "recommend" rather than "like" something makes people 32 percent more likely to take your suggestion. Using the word "whom" in online dating profiles makes men 31 percent more likely to get a date. Adding more prepositions to a cover letter makes you 24 percent more likely to get the job. And saying "is not" rather than "isn't" when describing a product makes people pay three dollars more to get it. The language used in earnings calls influences companies' stock price, and the language used by CEOs' impacts investment returns.

How do we know all this? From the new science of language. Technological advances in machine learning, computational linguistics, and natural language processing, combined with the digitization of everything from cover letters to conversations, have revolutionized our ability to analyze language, yielding unprecedented insights.

I started using automated text analysis by accident. In the mid-2000s, I was a first-year professor at the Wharton School, doing research on why things catch on. We were interested in why people talk about and share some things rather than others and had compiled a data set of thousands of *New York Times* articles, everything from front-page and world news to sports and lifestyle content. Many of the articles were great reads, but only a small portion made it onto the site's "most emailed" list, and we were trying to figure out why.

To find out, we needed to measure different reasons content might go viral. Maybe articles featured on the *Times* home page get more attention, for example, so we measured that. Similarly, maybe certain sections have more readers or certain writers have larger audiences, so we measured those things as well.

We were particularly interested in whether certain ways of writing might make articles more likely to be shared, but figuring that out required finding a way to measure features of the articles, like how much emotion each article evoked or how much useful information it contained. We started by enlisting research assistants. Interested undergraduates would email me asking if they could get involved with research, and this was an easy way they could help out. Each student would read an article and rate it on things like whether it evoked a little emotion or a lot.

This approach worked pretty well, at least initially. They coded a few articles and then a few dozen.

But applying this method to thousands of articles didn't work so well. It took time for a research assistant to read an article, and reading ten, a hundred, or a thousand articles took ten, a hundred, or a thousand times as long.

We hired a small army of research assistants, but even then, progress was slow. Further, the more people we hired, the less sure we were that we were getting consistent results. One research assistant might feel that a particular article was emotional, while another didn't, and we were worried that those inconsistencies would hurt our conclusions.

We needed an objective method that would scale. A consistent way to measure things across thousands of articles without making our research assistants tired and burnt out.

I started talking to some colleagues, and someone suggested a computer program called Linguistic Inquiry and Word Count. The program was brilliantly simple. Users inputted a block of text (e.g., newspaper article or anything else) and the program would spit out scores on various dimensions. By counting the number of emotion-related words appearing in an article, for example, the program gauged whether that article was more or less focused on emotion.

Unlike research assistants, the program never got tired. Further, it was perfectly consistent. It always coded things the same way.

Linguistic Inquiry and Word Count, or LIWC, as it is often known, became my favorite new research tool.*

WISDOM FROM WORDS

In the decades since then, hundreds of new tools and approaches have emerged. Methods for counting particular terms, discovering the main themes in a document, and extracting wisdom from words.

And just as the microscope revolutionized biology and the telescope upended astronomy, natural language processing tools have transformed the social sciences, providing insight into all types of human behavior. We've parsed customer service calls to uncover the words that increase customer satisfaction, dissected conversations to understand why some go better than others, and scrutinized online articles to identify writing that keeps readers engaged. We've examined thousands of movie scripts

---

* If you're interested in LIWC, check out James W. Pennebaker's excellent book, *The Secret Life of Pronouns*.

to determine why some become blockbusters, studied tens of thousands of academic papers to understand how to write for impact, and analyzed millions of online reviews to learn how language influences word of mouth.

We've parsed patient interactions to identify what increases medical adherence, dissected parole hearings to uncover what makes an effective apology, and examined legal arguments to discover what wins cases. We've scrutinized the scripts of tens of thousands of TV shows to figure out what makes a good story and analyzed over a quarter of a million song lyrics to identify what makes a hit.

Along the way, I've seen the power of magic words. Yes, what we say matters, but some words are more impactful than others. The right words, used at the right time, can change minds, engage audiences, and drive action.

So what are these magic words, and how can we take advantage of their power?

This book uncovers the hidden science behind how language works and more important, how we can use it more effectively. To persuade others, deepen relationships, and be more successful at home and at work.

Specifically, we'll discuss six types of magic words: words that (1) activate identity and agency, (2) convey confidence, (3) ask the right questions, (4) leverage concreteness, (5) employ emotion, and (6) harness similarity (and difference).

1: Activate Identity and Agency

Words suggest who's in charge, who's to blame, and what it means to engage in a particular action. Consequently, slight changes in the words we use can have a big impact. Discover why using nouns rather than verbs can help persuade others, how saying no the right way can help us achieve our goals, and how shifting just one word in the question we ask ourselves when we get stuck can help us be more creative. Why talking about ourselves in third person can reduce anxiety and make us better communicators, and why a simple word like "you" helps some social interactions but hurts others. How words impact agency and empathy, shifting whether people behave ethically, turn out to vote, or bicker with their spouse.

2: Convey Confidence

Words not only convey facts and opinions, they convey how confident we are in those facts and opinions, which shapes how we're perceived and our influence. Learn how getting rid of the wrong words turned a floundering sales executive into a top performer, why the way lawyers talk can be just as important as the facts they share, and the linguistic styles that make people seem more credible, trustworthy, and authoritative. Why people prefer confident financial advisers, even when they're more likely to be wrong, and why saying a restaurant "has" rather than "had" great food will make others more likely to go there. And while certainty is beneficial some of the time, I'll show you when uncertain language is more effective. Why expressing doubt about controversial topics can encourage the other side to listen and when acknowledging limitations can make communicators seem more trustworthy.

3: Ask the Right Questions

In this chapter, you'll learn about the science of asking questions. Why asking for advice makes people think you're smarter and why asking more questions make daters more likely to get a second date. Which types of questions are more effective and the right times to ask them. How to deflect difficult questions and encourage others to divulge sensitive information. How a married couple discovered a foolproof way for deepening social connection and why asking the right questions helps show people you care.

4: Leverage Concreteness

This chapter showcases the power of linguistic concreteness. Which words show listening and why talking about "fixing" rather than "solving" a problem improves customer satisfaction. Why knowledge can be a curse; and why talking about a "gray T-shirt" rather than a "top" increases sales. And lest you think it's always better to be concrete, I'll show you when it's better to be more abstract. Why abstract language signals power, leadership, and helps startups raise funding.

5: Employ Emotion

Chapter 5 explores why emotional language enhances engagement and how to harness it in all aspects of life. Discover how a twenty-two-year-old intern built a podcasting empire by understanding the science of what makes a good story, why adding negative things can actually make positive ones more enjoyable, and why using emotional language boosts sales in some product categories, but not others. You'll learn how to hold people's attention, even for topics that might not seem the most interesting, and why making people feel proud or happy may make them less likely to listen to whatever you have to say next. By the end of the chapter you'll understand how to leverage emotional language, when to use it, and how to engineer presentations, stories, and content to deeply engage any audience.

6: Harness Similarity (and Difference)

This chapter will teach you about the language of similarity. What linguistic similarity means and why it helps explain everything from who gets promoted or becomes friends to who gets fired or goes on a second date. But similarity isn't always good. Sometimes difference is better. Discover why atypical songs end up being more popular and how the artificial intelligence behind Siri and Alexa is being used to quantify how quickly stories move, and how much ground they cover. By the end you'll understand how to pick up on others' linguistic style, when to use language that is similar to or different from others', and how to present your ideas in ways that make them both easier to understand and more likely to generate a positive response.

7: What Language Reveals

The first six chapters focus on language's impact. How you can use it to be happier, healthier, and more successful. In the last chapter, I'll teach you some of the powerful things words reveal. Learn how researchers identified whether a play was written by Shakespeare without even reading it and how you can predict who will default on a loan based on the words they use in their application (hint: don't trust extraverts). You'll also discover what language reveals about society more broadly. How analyzing a quarter of a million songs answered the age-old question of whether music is misogynous (and whether it's gotten better over time) and how body camera footage showed the subtle biases that creep into the ways police talk to Black and White community members. By the end you'll be better able to use language to decode the world around you. Both what words reveal about other people and their motives, and how language reflects subtle societal stereotypes and biases.

Each chapter focuses on one type of magic words and how to use them. Some insights are as simple as saying "don't" rather than "can't"; others are more complex and context dependent.

Further, while the book focuses on how to use language more effectively, if you're interested in the tools used to discover these insights, check out the reference guide in the Appendix. It lists some of the main approaches, as well as how various companies, organizations, and industries can and have applied them.

Whether we realize it or not, we're all writers. We may not write books or news articles, or call ourselves authors or journalists, but we still write. We write emails to colleagues and texts to friends. We write reports for bosses and draft slide decks for clients.

We're also all public speakers. We may not go onstage in front of thousands of people, but we all speak in public. Whether making presentations to the company or chitchatting on a first date. Whether asking donors to make a pledge or asking the kids to clean up their rooms.

But to be better writers and speakers—to communicate with intention and care—we have to know the right words to use. It's hard to get people to listen, to pay attention, to persuade them to do what we want. And it's hard to motivate others, encourage creativity, and build social connections.

But the right words can help.

It's often said that certain people have a way with words. They're persuasive and charismatic, and it seems as though they always know the right thing to say. But are the rest of us who weren't born that way out of luck?

Not quite.

Because being a great writer or orator isn't something you're born with, it's something you can learn to do. Words have an amazing impact, and by understanding when, why, and how they work, we can use them to increase ours.

Whether you want to use language more effectively or just understand how it works, this book will show you how.

1

Activate Identity and Agency

Not far from the bustling venture capital firms that make up Silicon Valley, down an unassuming side street, lies what has been called one of the best preschools in the United States. Bing Nursery School is every child's dream. Each classroom has a half acre of outdoor space, complete with undulating mounds and bridges, sand pools, chicken coops, and rabbit hutches. Large, light-filled classrooms overflow with art supplies, blocks, and other materials designed to excite and enrich. Even the building itself was built with kids in mind, the windows extending down to little-kid level.

Not surprisingly, competition for admission is fierce. Thousands of anxious parents clamor to get onto the wait list for only a few hundred slots. Others try to persuade admissions officials of their child's genius, highlighting early musical ability or being able to count in multiple languages.

But Bing isn't looking for exceptional children; in fact, just the opposite. It prefers to recruit a diverse group of kids to reflect the population at large. Because Bing isn't just a school, it's also a laboratory.

In the early 1960s, Stanford University was looking to build a new lab school. Faculty and staff needed child care, and graduate students in education and psychology needed hands-on learning opportunities, so with a grant from the National Science Foundation, Stanford built a state-of-the-art research facility. In addition to the welcoming indoor and outdoor spaces that make Bing a model nursery school, one-way mirrors in classrooms and separate observation spaces make it an ideal place for researchers to study child development.

Since then, hundreds of studies have been run at Bing. Bing was the site of the so-called "Marshmallow Test," for example, which examined children's ability to delay gratification (i.e., wait to eat the marshmallow in front of you and get a second one later). Similarly, work on intrinsic motivation found that rewarding children for something they already enjoyed doing (i.e., coloring) actually made it less likely for them to do it in the future.

More recently, a group of scientists went to Bing to explore how to encourage kids to help out.[1] It goes without saying that helping is valuable. Parents ask kids to help clean up their dishes, teachers ask kids to help put away their toys, and peers ask kids for help pushing them on the swing.

But as anyone who's ever tried to get kids to do something can attest, they don't always want to help. Just like clients, colleagues, and customers, kids aren't always interested in doing what we want them to do. They'd rather be stacking Magna-Tiles, jumping on the couch, or unlacing the shoelaces of all the shoes in the hall closet.

To try to understand how to persuade kids and others, the scientists asked a group of four- and five-year-olds to do something kids are particularly reticent to do: help tidy up. A pile of blocks on the floor needed to be put into a container, toys needed to be put away, and an overturned cup of crayons needed to be cleaned up. Further, to make persuasion even more difficult, the scientists waited until the kids were already engaged in some other activity—playing with toys or drawing with crayons—before they were asked. So they'd be particularly uninterested in lending a hand.

Some of the kids were simply asked to help. They were reminded that helping is good and that it involves everything from picking things up to lending a hand whenever others are in need.

But for another group of children, the scientists tried an interesting intervention. The kids received almost exactly the same speech. Same spiel about helping others and different ways to help. But one detail was different. Rather than asking the kids to "help," the scientists asked them to be a "helper" instead.

This difference seems negligible. So small that you might not have even noticed it. And in many ways, it is. Both requests involved the same content (i.e., picking stuff up), and both involve the word "help" in one form or another. In fact, the difference is basically only two letters (adding -*er* on the end).

And yet, even though the change might seem minor, it made a big difference. Compared to simply asking kids to help, asking kids to be a help*er* increased helping by almost a third.

Why? Why did two letters have such a big impact?

The answer, it turns out, has to do with the difference between verbs and nouns.

TURNING ACTIONS INTO IDENTITIES

Imagine I told you about two people, Rebecca and Fred. Rebecca goes running, and Fred is a runner. Who do you think likes running more?

People can be described in various ways. Peter is old, and Scott is young. Susan is female, and Tom is male. Charlie likes baseball, Kristen is a liberal, and Mike eats a lot of chocolate. Jessica is a morning person, Danny loves dogs, and Jill is a coffee drinker. From demographics like age and gender, to opinions, traits, and preferences, descriptions like these provide some sense of who someone is or what they're like.

There are many ways, however, to say the same thing. Someone who has left-leaning political beliefs, for example, could be described as being "liberal" or as being "a liberal." Someone who likes dogs a lot could be described as "loving dogs" or as being "a dog lover." These may seem like small variations, but in each case, the latter describes a category. If someone is described as liberal, it suggests that they hold left-leaning beliefs. But describing someone as "a liberal" suggests that they fall into a particular group or type. They are a member of a specific set of people.

Category labels often imply a degree of permanence or stability. Rather than noting what someone did or does, feels or felt, category labels hint at a deeper essence: Who someone *is*. Regardless of time or situation, this is the type of person they are. That they will always be that way.

While saying someone is liberal suggests that they currently hold left-leaning beliefs, saying they are *a* liberal suggests something more permanent. While saying someone loves dogs suggest they currently feel that way, saying they are a dog lover suggest they are a certain type of person and will be that way forever more. Things that could be seen as temporary states (e.g., "Sally didn't put the dishes away"), for example, often seem more enduring or fundamental when expressed using category labels (i.e., "Sally is a slob"). Losing is bad. Being a loser is even worse.

Indeed, when told someone named Rose "eats a lot of carrots," for example, describing her as a "carrot-eater" led observers to think that aspect of Rose's disposition was more stable. They thought Rose was more likely to eat lots of carrots when she was younger, more likely to eat lots of carrots in the future, and more likely to eat carrots even if other people tried to stop her from doing it. Regardless of past or future, and opposition or not, the behavior would persist.[2]

Inferences from labels can be so strong that people are often careful to separate labels from the behaviors they describe. When arguing for leniency for a client, for example, a lawyer may say, "He's not a criminal; he just made a bad decision." Similarly, a sports fan may say, "I watch some games, but I'm not a fanatic."

In all these cases, labels involve a particular part of speech: nouns. The trait "liberal" is an adjective, but the category "a liberal" is a noun. Saying that someone "runs a lot" uses "run" as a verb, while saying someone is "a runner" turns that action (a verb) into an identity (a noun).

Across a variety of topics and domains, research finds that turning actions into identities can shape how others are perceived.[3] Hearing someone is a coffee drinker (rather than drinks coffee a lot), for example, or is a PC person (rather than uses PCs a lot), led observers to infer that this person liked coffee (or PCs) more, was more likely to hold that preference in the future, and more likely to adhere to it even if others around them didn't feel the same.

Changing a verb-based description (e.g., "drinks coffee") to a noun (e.g., "is a coffee drinker") made it seem like that person's attitudes or preferences were more dispositional, and thus stronger and more stable.

Part of someone's identity, rather than just an attitude they happen to hold.

The fact that turning actions into identities shapes how people are perceived has a number of useful applications. Describing oneself as a hard work*er* on a résumé, for example, rather than as hard work*ing* should lead to more favorable impressions. Describing our coworkers as innovat*ors* rather than as innovat*ive* should have positive effects on how they're perceived.

But the effects are even broader. Because beyond just impacting perceptions, the same underlying ideas can be used to change *behavior*. By framing actions as a way to claim desired identities or selves, turning actions into identities can actually shift the actions others take.

Everyone wants to see themselves positively: as intelligent, competent, attractive, and efficacious. Some of us may care about being athletic, good at trivia, or able to make a delicious dinner out of whatever happens to be in the fridge, but in general, we all want to see ourselves in a positive light. Consequently, we try to act in ways that support how we want to see ourselves. Want to feel athletic? Better go for a run once in a while. Want to feel rich or high status? Better buy that fancy car or take that exotic vacation. By taking consistent actions and avoiding inconsistent ones, we can signal to ourselves that we are the type of person we want to be.

But this is where it gets interesting, because if people want to look certain ways, then framing certain actions as opportunities to confirm desired identities can encourage them to behave accordingly. And that's where the Bing Nursery School study comes in.

When we ask people to help, we often use verbs: "Can you *help* clean up the blocks?" or "Can you *help* with the dishes?" Both use the action verb "help" to make the request. But the same request can be rephrased by turning the verb into a noun. Rather than asking for *help* cleaning up the blocks, for example, try using a noun instead: "Can you be a *helper* and clean up the blocks?" This simple shift turns what was previously just an action (i.e., helping) into something more profound. Now picking up blocks isn't just helping, it's an opportunity. An opportunity to claim a desired identity.

Some parents might find this hard to believe, but most kids want to see themselves as helpers. Sure, they can't take out the trash or cook dinner, but being a helper, contributing to the group, is a positive identity they'd like to embrace. So naming the verb, or turning it into a noun, turns what would otherwise just be an action (helping) into an opportunity to claim a positive identity (being a helper). Now picking up blocks is a chance for me to show myself, and maybe even someone else, that I'm a good person. That I'm a member of this desirable group.

Helping? Sure that's fine. But getting the chance to see oneself as a helper? An identity I like the idea of being part of? Now that's worth putting down the crayons for and helping to clean up. Which is exactly what the kids at Bing did.

The impact of turning verbs into nouns goes far beyond kids and cleaning up. In 2008, for example, researchers used the same principle to increase voter turnout. Voting is key to a functioning democracy and a chance to shape how the country is run, yet many people still don't do it. Just like helping, voting is something people know they should do but don't always follow through on. They're too busy, they forget, or they just don't care enough about the candidates involved to cast a ballot.

Researchers wondered if language could help. Specifically, rather than the standard communication approach (asking people to vote), they tried something slightly different: They talked about being a vote*r*. Again, the difference seems minuscule. Essentially adding the letter *r* to the end of the word "vote." But the change worked. It boosted voter turnout by over 15 percent.[4]

Rephrasing a behavior—voting—to be an opportunity to claim a positive identity—voter—led more people to engage in the behavior. Turning the mere act of voting into a chance to express something positive about themselves led more people to take that action.

Want people to listen? Ask them to be a listen*er*. Want them to lead? Ask them to be a lead*er*. Want them to work harder? Encourage them to be a top performer.*

The same idea can even be used to encourage people to avoid negative behaviors. Dishonesty is costly. Workplace crime, for example, costs US businesses over more than $50 billion a year.

But although people are often encouraged to behave ethically or do the right thing, identity language may be more effective. Indeed, research finds that rather than saying "Don't cheat," saying "Don't be a cheat*er*" more than halved the amount of cheating.[5] People were less likely to cheat when doing so would signal they held an undesirable identity.

Trying to get people to stop littering? Rather than saying "Please don't litter," say "Please don't be a litterbug." Trying to get kids to tell

---

* As with any useful approach, there are situations in which doing this might backfire. Compared to telling kids that a science-related game involved "doing science," for example, telling them that the game involved "being scientists" reduced girls' interest in the game. The authors speculated that identity "language could lead to problematic consequences if children have reason to question whether they themselves are the kind of people who fit into the scientist category (e.g., after experiencing setbacks in science or developing stereotypes about scientists), because children might disengage if they no longer view science as consistent with their own identities." See Marjorie Rhodes et al., "Subtle Linguistic Cues Increase Girls' Engagement in Science," *Psychological Science* 30, no. 3 (2019): 455–66, https://doi.org/10.1177/0956797618823670.

the truth? Rather than saying "Don't lie," saying "Don't be a liar" should be more effective.

These ideas can even be applied to oneself. Trying to get into the habit of exercising or running more often? Telling people that you're a runn*er*, rather than saying you run, should make running seem like a more stable, consistent part of who you are and increase your likelihood of sticking with it.

Turning actions into identities, though, is just one way to apply a broader category of language. And that is the language of identity and agency.

Four more ways to harness it are to: (1) change *can't*s to *don't*s, (2) turn *should*s into *could*s, (3) talk to yourself, and (4) know when to use "you."

CHANGE *CAN'T*S TO *DON'T*S

The fact that language can encourage desired actions is intriguing. Beyond just desired selves, though, language also does something else. It indicates who is in control.

Everyone has goals they're trying to achieve. Exercise more and lose a little weight. Get out of debt or get those finances in order. Get more organized, learn something new, or spend more time with friends and family.

But while we all have goals, and work hard to achieve them, we often fall short. We mean to exercise more, or get those finances in order, but it doesn't happen.

And temptation is a big reason why. We mean to eat healthier, but our colleagues are going out for pizza, and it looks too good to pass up. We mean to get more organized but get sucked into a friend's social media feed and two hours later have no idea where the time went. Despite our best efforts to make New Year's resolutions, or turn over a new leaf, temptation gets in the way.

Could words help?

When faced with temptation, we often use the word "can't." That deep-dish pizza looks delicious, but I *can't* have any because I'm trying to eat healthier. I'd love to go on vacation with you, but I *can't* because I'm trying to save money. We default to *can't* because it's an easy way to describe why we're not able to do something.

In 2010, though, two consumer psychologists asked people who were interested in healthier eating to participate in an experiment about ways to do so more effectively.[6] Participants were told that each time they were faced with temptation they should try a specific strategy to avoid giving in. Half the people were asked to take the normal approach of saying "I can't." When tempted by chocolate cake, for example, they would say something like "I can't eat chocolate cake" either to themselves or to others.

Other people, however, were asked to take a slightly different approach: rather than saying "I can't" when trying to ward off temptation, they were encouraged to say, "I don't." When tempted by chocolate cake, for example, they would say something such as "I don't eat chocolate cake" to themselves or others.

Just like the difference between help and help*er*, the difference between "can't" and "don't" might seem tiny. And it is. Both are four letters long, and both are easy ways to say no that we all use frequently.

But it turned out that one word was a lot more effective than the other. After answering a few questions, and completing an unrelated experiment, participants got up to leave the room. And as they turned in their survey, they were offered a choice between two snacks as thanks for coming in: either a candy bar or a healthier granola bar.

The candy bars looked delicious. Indeed, around 75 percent of people who practiced saying "I can't" ended up picking one. But among people who practiced saying "I don't," the number of people picking the candy bar was cut in half. Saying "I don't" rather than "I can't" more than doubled people's ability to avoid temptation and stick to their goals.

When the scientists dug further, they found that saying "I don't" was more effective because of the way it made people feel.

Saying "I can't" suggests we're unable do something, but it also suggests a particular type of reason why. To get a sense of what it is, try filling in the following statements.

I can't eat _____ because _____.

I can't buy _____ because _____.

I can't do _____ because _____.

Regardless of what food, action, or thing you listed, what you wrote down after the word "because" was probably some sort of external constraint. I can't eat deep-dish pizza *because* my doctor told me I should eat healthier. I can't buy a new television *because* my spouse wants me to save money.

Saying "I can't" often implies that we *want* to do the thing but something or someone else is getting in the way. Some external constraint (e.g., a doctor, spouse, or something else) is stopping us from doing what we'd like to do.

Saying "I don't," however, suggests something quite different. When asked to complete "I don't" statements, the type of reasons people list change dramatically. Try filling in the following statements.

I don't eat _____ because _____.

I don't buy _____ because _____.

I don't _____ because _____.

Rather than being some temporary constraint, now the driver of saying no is something more permanent; it's an entrenched attitude.

And rather than being external, or someone else or something else that is preventing us from doing what we want, now the locus of control is more internal. I don't eat deep-dish pizza because *I* don't like it that much. I don't check my email every five minutes because *I*'d rather get some deep thinking done.

Saying "I don't" helped people avoid temptation because it made them feel empowered. Like they were in control. Rather than something else getting in the way of something they wanted to do, they were in the driver's seat. It was up to them. Sure, I could binge-watch, spend frivolously, or fritter time away, but *I*'d rather not. *I*'d prefer to be doing something else.

And this feeling of empowerment made it easier for them to turn down temptation. After all, those goals were theirs in the first place.

Having a tough time sticking with that New Year's resolution? Struggling to stick to a goal? Try saying "I don't" rather than "I can't."

Try writing down why you don't do the thing you're trying to avoid, taking care to focus on the reasons that make you feel in control. If you're worried that you'll forget, put the "I don't" statement on a sticky note and place it somewhere like on the fridge or your computer so that you'll see it when temptation strikes. Or put it into a calendar invite that will pop up around the time when you know your resolve will be tested. Seeing that reminder will encourage you to remember that you're in control and make it easier to stick to your goals.

The same tactic can be applied to other types of refusals. Sometimes people ask us to do things that we want to say no to, but it's hard to find a polite way to decline. It's good to be helpful or supportive, but we can't do it all. When a coworker asks us to serve on a task force that's completely unrelated to our job or a boss asks us to do something that's beyond the scope of what we've agreed on, it can be tough to find a way out.

Experts often suggest finding a "no buddy." A colleague, superior, or someone else who can provide an external source of the refusal.

But language can help us do the same thing.

In situations like these, "can't" can be a particularly useful word. While "can't" isn't as effective in avoiding temptation because it suggests the driver of behavior is external, this same reason actually makes it particularly useful for turning down unwanted requests.

Saying you *can't* serve on the task force because your boss asked you to mentor a new hire, or that you *can't* go beyond the agreed-upon scope because it will delay the final product distances you from the refusal. It's not *you* saying no because *you* didn't want to be helpful, it's another, external thing getting in the way. *You* want to help, but the other thing prevents you.

In fact, in cases where the other party has control over the external constraint, making it clear that the constraint is the barrier can help make you both better off. You can't do both things, but by making it clear what the external constraint is, you give the other person the opportunity to decide which thing is more important. They may end up finding someone else to help, or they may work with you to move the external roadblock.

TURN *SHOULD*S INTO *COULD*S

It's tough to be creative. Although 60 percent of CEOs in one study said that creativity is the most important leadership quality, 75 percent of people think they're not living up to their creative potential.

One key place creativity is particularly important is when it comes to problem solving.

Imagine that your pet has fallen ill with a rare kind of cancer. You get different opinions, and it appears that there seems to be only one drug that might save their life. Fortunately, the company that makes the drug is located near where you live. Unfortunately, the drug is extremely expensive.

You look into taking out loans, getting extra credit cards, and asking friends and family to borrow money, but you're only able pull together half of what the treatment costs. You get desperate and consider breaking into the factory to steal the drug.

Moral dilemmas, like whether to steal a drug for a sick pet, can often be characterized as ethical challenges between right and wrong. Whether you should cheat to get ahead, for example, even if no one will find out, or lie to save money, even though you won't get caught.

In situations like these, there is a clear correct answer. Even though no one will find out, cheating is bad. Even if you won't get caught, lying is wrong. Sure, there's a conflict between self-interest and something else, but the "right" thing to do is pretty clear.

In other situations, however, the "right" answer, if there even is one, is less obvious. In the case of the cancer-stricken pet, for example, neither option is ideal. Stealing is clearly wrong, but just letting your poor pet waste away doesn't seem right, either.

Situations like these are often called "right-versus-right" dilemmas because they involve tradeoffs between moral imperatives. We're caught in a conflict that requires sacrificing one principle (e.g., acting fairly and ethically) for another (e.g., upholding our duty to a loved one). Choosing one seems like forgoing the other, so rather than a win-win, it feels more like a lose-lose.

When contemplating such challenges, we often ask ourselves a classic question: What *should* I do? Should I help my pet (but violate the imperative not to steal) or stay within the law (but not save a valued companion)?

We think in *should*s all the time. Instruction manuals tell us how we *should* use products, employee handbooks tell us what we *should* do at the office, and corporate codes of conduct clarify what the organization *should* do regarding diversity or the environment.

Not surprisingly, then, when faced with challenges, moral or otherwise, we often think about what we *should* do. Indeed, when asked to provide the word or phrase that best captured what they were thinking as they considered their response to different moral dilemmas, people said something like what they should do almost two-thirds of the time.

But while shoulds are common, thinking in shoulds can often get us stuck. Shoulds are great for resolving questions of right and wrong. Whether to lie, cheat, or steal, even if it doesn't seem like a big deal and no one else will find out. Thinking about what one should do in these situations reminds us of our moral compass. It encourages us to think about what we "ought" to do, and in so doing, helps us choose the morally right path.

In many other situations, though, shoulds are less helpful. When thinking about whether to steal the drug to save your sick pet, a should mindset doesn't get us very far because there is no "right" answer. Thinking in shoulds digs us deeper and deeper into trading off between two things that feel less than ideal. This mindset forces us to weigh different values against one another, settling for the least undesirable option, and often feeling quite stuck.

But there's a better way.

Whether trying to solve a moral dilemma, or think creatively more generally, we're often looking for a flash of insight. A eureka moment where a solution, or even just how we see the problem, suddenly becomes clear. Indeed, rather than occurring immediately, or resulting from deep analysis and deliberation, insight often strikes like a lightning bolt when we least expect it.

In creativity, for example, insight strikes when we see a problem differently. Think about fixing a lit candle to the wall using only a box of matches and a box of thumbtacks. Take a moment to think about this problem. How would you solve it?

When people try to devise an answer, they often jump right to the thumbtacks. They try to use the thumbtacks to fix the candle to the wall.

Unfortunately, though, this doesn't work. The tacks aren't big enough and there's no way to use them to attach the candle. So people try again and again, using different configurations and failing repeatedly.

But looked at differently, the thumbtacks can be quite useful. Rather than trying to tack the candle directly to the wall, use the thumbtack box instead. Empty out the thumbtacks, use them to secure the box to the wall, and then use the box as a stand for the lit candle.

Problem solved.

Solutions like these, though, require relaxing one's assumptions. Rather than seeing the objects as having fixed functions (i.e., the thumbtack box's job is to hold the tacks), taking a broader perspective and thinking how they could be used differently.

To explore how to get to insight, some researchers from Harvard conducted an experiment.[7] They put together different moral dilemmas, similar to the sick pet, and examined how people solved them.

And to see whether they could increase creative problem solving, they had one group of people approach the problems slightly differently. Rather than taking the default approach, or thinking about what one *should* do, the researchers asked them to think about what they *could* do instead.

This simple shift made a big difference. People who thought about what they *could* do came up with much better solutions. They were higher quality and three times as creative.

Rather than getting bogged down in which of two imperfect options was best, asking people to think about what they *could* do encouraged them to bring a different mindset to the problem. To take a step back, get some distance from the situation, and think more broadly. To consider multiple objectives, alternatives, and outcomes. To recognize that there might be other possibilities.

Rather than black and white, or either/or, *could* encouraged people to realize that there might be alternate paths. Rather than irreconcilable choices between saving the pet and stealing, there might be other, potentially better directions. Offering to work for free for the drugmaker (or veterinarian) to pay for the drug, or trying a GoFundMe campaign to raise money for the treatment.

"Could " led to more innovative solutions because it encouraged divergent thinking. Thinking outside the box and without boundaries. Considering multiple approaches, encouraging new connections, and reducing the likelihood of settling for obvious answers. Rather than just seeing things for how they are, thinking in terms of *"could"* encourages us to see them for how they *could* be. To overlook the obvious and ex-plore different ways of doing things.

When faced with needing to erase a pencil mark, for example, people who considered what objects *could* be were more likely to come up with clever uses for ordinary things.[8] When they needed to erase a pencil mark, for example, and they didn't have access to an eraser, they recognized that a rubber band could serve the same function. Similarly, when needing a mask to avoid inhaling noxious dust, people who thought about what objects *could* do were more likely to recognize they could use a sock to do the same job.

Stuck on a tough problem? Want to be more creative or encourage creativity in others?

Foster a *could* mindset. Rather than thinking about what *should* be done, ask what *could* be done instead. Doing so encourages us and others to take agency, consider new paths, and turn roadblocks into opportunities.

The same holds when asking others for advice. When asking for help, we tend to do so in a specific way: we ask people what they think we *should* do.

Though this makes sense in some ways, it's not always the best approach. Asking what they think we *could* do will encourage them to think more broadly and give us better, more creative direction.

TALK TO YOURSELF

So far, we've highlighted several ways language can be used to activate identity and agency. How to persuade people to do something by making it a way they can approach a desired identity or avoid an undesired one. How to avoid temptation by empowering ourselves to feel like we're in control. And how to be more creative by focusing on what we can do rather than what external constraints might suggest.

In some instances, though, using language to distance ourselves from something can actually be the better approach.

It's the night before a big presentation and you can't sleep. You feel like you know the material pretty well, but a lot is riding on how things go tomorrow, so you want to make sure to get it right. You've gone over the slides at least a half-dozen times, adding a bullet point here and tweaking language there, but you're still feeling anxious.

In situations like these, how can we reduce anxiety and perform our best?

When making a big presentation, going on a first date, or having a difficult conversation, our nerves often run rampant. We're worried about making a mistake, saying the wrong thing, or performing poorly. That worrying makes it even worse. We ruminate on everything that could go wrong and focus so much on the negative possibilities that it ends up interfering with our performance.

Thankfully, other people often intervene. Friends, partners, or close colleagues sense our anxiety and work to help calm us down. "You'll do great," they say, or "Don't worry about it, you're always such a persuasive speaker and you're super prepared." They help us look on the bright side, tell us that everything will be okay, or remind us how well we did last time. Focusing our attention on positive aspects or what we can control.

One question is why we can't seem to do the same thing for ourselves. After all, if other people telling us we'll do great is enough to calm us down, why can't we just tell ourselves the same thing?

One possibility is that our problems are just bigger than other people's. Our presentations, first dates, or difficult conversations are just more important, nerve wracking, or difficult than the ones that other people are dealing with.

Possibly. But unless we're presenting at the White House, or negotiating a nuclear arms treaty, our difficulties are probably on par with everyone else's.

Instead, the issue is actually something more subtle. Because even when faced with exactly the same situation, it feels different when it's happening to us.

When someone else is anxious or nervous, it's easy to give them useful advice. To step back, take a broader vantage point, and reason through things in a rational manner. Seeing the situation more objectively.

Should that presentation really be so anxiety-provoking? Probably not. Will it be the end of the world? Unlikely. Overall, in the grand scheme of things, it's not really as terrifying as one might think.

But when it's happening to us, it's hard to get that distance. We're so caught up in the situation that we can't think straight. Our emotions run wild and get the best of us. Attention narrows, we ruminate on the negative, and can't seem to break free.

To explore ways to calm people down, researchers from the University of Michigan put subjects into a stressful situation.[9] They were asked to think about their dream job, the position they'd always wanted at the company they'd always hoped to work for.

Then they were asked to give a speech about why they were qualified for that role. You have to stand up in front of a group of evaluators and explain why out of the hundreds, if not thousands, of people who might want the position, they were the right person for the job.

As if that weren't challenging enough, they were given only five minutes to prepare.

Sound stressful? It was. People's heart rates surged, their blood pressure rose, and their level of cortisol, the body's main stress hormone, spiked. Giving a public speech in front of an audience that is evaluating you turns out to be one of the most powerful ways scientists can induce stress.

The researchers put people in this situation because they were interested in the impact of so-called self-talk. We use language to communicate with others, but we also use it to talk to ourselves. We tell ourselves to give it one last push when we're out for a tough run or complain to ourselves about the gray hairs that keep popping up every time we look closely in the mirror.

Self-talk is one's natural, internal dialogue. An inner voice that combines conscious thoughts and unconscious beliefs and biases. These words can be cheerful and supportive ("Give it one more go!") or negative and self-defeating ("Another gray hair? You must be getting old!").

The scientists wondered whether shifting people's approach to self-talk might help them better manage stress. So they gave people five minutes to prepare their speech and gave them one of two sets of instructions about how to use language to deal with anxiety .

People usually talk to themselves in the first person. When trying to understand our feelings or sort out why we're feeling anxious, we ask ourselves questions like "Why am *I* so upset?" or "What's causing *me* to feel this way?" We use words like "I," "me," or "my" (all first-person pronouns) to refer to ourselves.

One group of people were told to stick with this standard approach. They were asked to use first-person pronouns when trying to understand their feelings and to ask themselves questions like "Why do *I* feel this way?" or "What are the underlying causes and reasons for *my* feelings?"

The other group used language to take a slightly different perspective.

Rather than trying to understand their anxiety from their own vantage point, they were asked to take an outsider's perspective. Rather than referring to themselves using "*I*" or "*me*," they were encouraged to talk to themselves like someone else would, using words like "*you*," their name, or "*he*" or "*she*" instead.

If the person's name was Jane, for example, she asked herself questions like "Why does *Jane* feel this way? Why is *she* anxious about the speech? What are the causes and reasons for *Jane's* feelings?"

Participants read the instructions, took a minute to reflect on their feelings, and then went to another room to deliver their speech. Evaluators watched their speeches and graded them on a number of dimensions.

The results were striking. Both groups of speakers had the same difficult experience. They were put into the same tough situation (giving a public speech), given the same minimal amount of time to prepare, and given the same five minutes to think about their feelings before giving their speech. The only difference was whether they talked to themselves in the second or third person rather than first person. Whether they asked themselves things like "Why are *you* so upset" rather than "Why am *I* so upset."

But using different words had a big effect on performance. Compared to normal self-talk words like "*I*" or "*me*," taking an outsider's perspective (i.e., using one's own name or words like "*you*") helped people give better speeches. They were more confident, less nervous, and performed better overall.

This linguistic shift helped people distance themselves from the difficult situation and see it more like an outsider would. People who took the normal "I" focused approach would say things like, "Oh, my god, how am I going do this? I can't prepare a speech in five minutes without notes. It takes days for me to prepare a speech!"

But using their first names, or words like "you," "he," or "she" encouraged them to think like an outsider and see the situation more positively. Rather than complaining or stressing themselves out even more, it encouraged them to provide support and advice: "Jane, you can do this. You've given a ton of speeches before."

Outsider language helped speakers see things more objectively, making the situation less anxiety-inducing. They felt fewer negative emotions and appraised the situation in more positive terms. More as a challenge that they could cope with, or rise up to meet, rather than a threat that they felt unprepared for or overwhelmed by.

And similar effects have been found in other domains. Whether choosing food, or considering a health scare, shifting away from first person language encouraged better outcomes by distancing people from the situation.[10] It led them to choose healthier food, or focus on the facts. By encouraging people to think about themselves as an outsider would, shifting language made them better off.

The same principle can be applied to a host of situations. Practicing positive self-talk, for example, helps athletes perform better.[11] Professional athletes often imagine success, practice multiple scenarios, or even repeat a mantra during training.

When trying to pump themselves up for competition, for example, athletes often tell themselves, "You can do it!" Saying "I can do it!" can feel a bit forced, but taking an outsider's perspective feels more natural and may be easier to apply.

KNOW WHEN TO USE "YOU"

More generally, the self-talk research highlights when pronouns like *you* are useful and when they're likely to backfire.

A few years ago, a multinational tech company asked me to analyze its social media posts to figure out what was working and what wasn't. After doing text analysis on thousands of posts, we found that using "you" increased readers' engagement. Posts that used the word "you" or other second-person pronouns such as "your" or "yourself" were liked more and received more comments.

The company started adjusting its social media strategy as a result. Using more of these words in their posts, and seeing a nice increase in subsequent engagement.

In addition, the company asked me to perform a similar analysis on customer support articles. Pages on this website about how to set up a new laptop or troubleshoot a device, and whether readers found those support pages helpful or not.

Compared to social media posts, though, on customer support pages words like "you" had the opposite effect. While words like "you" increased engagement on social media, it led customer support pages to be rated as *less* helpful, not more.

Intrigued, we started to explore the discrepancy.

Social media posts differ from support pages in numerous ways. They're shorter, less detailed, and more likely to be visited by non-users.

But to really understand why "you" worked differently, we realized the importance of understanding what "you," and other second-person pronouns, are doing in each context.

On social media, people's feeds are overflowing with content, and it's hard to get them to give anything a deeper look. Pictures help, but so does using the right words. In situations like these, words like "you" can act as a stop sign, flagging something as worthy of attention.

When someone sees a post titled "5 tips to save money" it's not clear whether it's relevant to them or not. But add the word "you" e.g., "5 tips *you* can use to save money," and suddenly the post seems much more personally relevant. This isn't just any information, this is something *you're* going to find useful. Even though the information itself hasn't changed.

"You" draws attention, increases relevance, and makes readers feel like someone is speaking directly to them.[12]

On customer support pages, however, drawing attention isn't as necessary because people are already there. They went to the support page because they have a question, or a problem they're trying to solve, so their attention is already focused on the content.

Further, though the use of "you" can suggest that information is personally relevant to the reader, it can also suggest responsibility or blame. Compared to saying "If the printer isn't working . . ." saying "If *you* can't get the printer to work . . ." suggests that the printer's not working is somehow the user's fault. That the problem lies not with the printer, but with the user who can't seem to get it to do what it's supposed to.[13]

Similarly, compared to more passive voice ("Space can be freed up by . . ."), active voice ("*You* can free up space by . . .") suggests that the user needs to do the work. And the more times the word "you" is used, the more work the user has to do.

Not surprisingly, then, while "you" helps on social media by drawing attention, it hurts on customer support pages, where it can suggest the user is at fault or to blame.

More generally, as we've discussed throughout the chapter, words can change who is in control: who is in charge, in the driver's seat, or responsible, in both good ways and bad.

Questions like "Did you feed the dog?" or "Did you check when the paperwork is due?" can feel accusatory. The intent may be benign, just a request for information, but they can easily be interpreted negatively. Who said it was my responsibility, or why wouldn't I have taken care of it?

A subtle shift in phrasing ("Has the dog had dinner?") is less likely to generate blowback. By focusing on the action rather than the actor, it removes any suggestion of reproach. I'm not suggesting that it's *your* job, I just want to find out whether it happened so I can do it if it hasn't.

The same goes for statements like "I wanted to talk but you were busy." The statement may be true. We wanted to talk, and the other person was busy. But phrasing it that way suggests that the other person is to blame. That not only is it bad they were busy, but it's their fault the conversation didn't occur.

Dropping the "you" and switching to something like "I wanted to talk, but now didn't seem like the best time," avoids any finger-pointing. Now it's clear that it's no one's fault, and we seem caring rather than demanding. Avoiding accusatory "you"s helps avoid placing unintended blame.

The same holds for "I," "me," and other first-person pronouns. After taking a first bite of food, a friend's three-year-old complained that "Dinner isn't yummy."

His parents, who had spent hours planning, shopping for, and cooking the meal, were obviously disappointed. They wanted their son to like the food. But they also took it as a chance to teach him an important lesson. They noted that there was a difference between something not being good and someone not liking it, and they said that just because one person doesn't like something doesn't mean it's bad.

When first-person pronouns are dropped, opinions can seem like they are being stated as fact. "This isn't right" or "Dinner isn't yummy" suggests that something is objectively bad. But adding "I" clarifies that the comment is meant to be stated as an opinion rather than fact.

the third person ("You can do it!"). It distances us from tough situations, reducing anxiety and increasing performance.

5. **Pick your pronouns.** And whether trying to get someone's attention, or not fight with a spouse, think carefully about how to use pronouns like "I" and "you." They can draw attention and take ownership, but they also suggest responsibility and blame.

By understanding the language of identity, and deploying it at the right time, we can use magic words to our advantage.

Beyond identity and agency, though, there's another type of magic word that deserves attention. And that is words that convey confidence.

2

Convey Confidence

When people think of famous orators, Donald Trump isn't usually the first name that comes to mind.

The Roman statesman Cicero is often lauded as one of the greatest speakers ever. He considered public speaking the highest form of intellectual activity and believed that good presenters should speak wisely and eloquently with a restrained, dignified delivery. Similarly, speakers like Abraham Lincoln and Winston Churchill were praised for their clear, logical argumentation, strong thoughts, and well-reasoned ideas.

Trump doesn't fit that stereotype. His sentences are usually grammatically awkward, repetitive, and filled with highly simplistic words. Take his remarks when announcing his presidential campaign: "I would build a great wall, and nobody builds walls better than me, believe me, and I'll build them very inexpensively," he said. "Our country is in serious trouble," he went on. "We don't have victories anymore. We used to have victories, but we don't have them. When was the last time anybody saw us beating, let's say, China, in a trade deal? I beat China all the time. All the time."

Not surprisingly, the speech was met with widespread derision. People panned it for being simplistic, *Time* magazine called it "empty," and others laughed it off as pure bluster.

Less than a year later, Trump was elected president of the United States.

Trump's speaking style is a far cry from what people usually think of as eloquent. His rambling, often incoherent manner is filled with disjointed thoughts, starts and stops, and a range of disfluencies.

But love him or hate him, Trump is a great salesman. He's convincing, persuasive, and amazingly impactful at motivating his audiences to action.

So, how does he do it?

To understand what makes Trump's speaking style so effective, it helps to start in a very different place. And that is in a small courtroom in Durham County, North Carolina

SPEAKING WITH POWER

Even if you've never sat in a courtroom, you've probably seen one on television. Lawyers for each side, congregating around large wooden desks. Witnesses taking the oath to tell the truth, the whole truth, and nothing but the truth. And a judge, wearing a plain black robe, sitting behind a raised desk, solemnly presiding over the proceedings.

Courtrooms are places where language matters a lot. It's impossible to travel back in time, so words are used to convey what occurred. They lay out what happened, who did what when, and where a suspect or key individual was at a particular time. Words determine guilt and innocence. Who goes to jail and who gets set free. Who is responsible and who is not.

In the early 1980s, anthropologist William O'Barr wondered whether presentation style might impact legal outcomes.[1] Whether beyond what was said, *how* it was said might be equally impactful.

The common assumption was that substance was all that mattered. Sure, a witness's testimony or lawyer's arguments drives the jury's decision, but that's simply because they laid out the facts. After all, the legal system is supposed to be an objective, unbiased arbiter of truth.

But O'Barr wondered whether that assumption might be wrong. He was interested in whether minor variations in linguistic style might impact how people were perceived and decisions were made. Whether subtle shifts in the words witnesses used, for example, might influence how their testimony was evaluated or the jury's overall decision on the case.

So for ten weeks one summer, he and his team observed and recorded trials. Misdemeanors, felonies, and all sorts of different cases. More than 150 hours of courtroom speech in total.

Then, they listened to the recordings, and transcribed what had been said.

When O'Barr analyzed the data, something stood out. Judges, lawyers, and expert witnesses talked differently from ordinary people such as regular witnesses and defendants. Sure, they used more legalese such as "habeas corpus" or "in pari delicto," but the difference was greater than that; the *way* they talked was different.

Judges, lawyers, and experts used less formal language ("please" or "yes, sir"), fewer filler words ("uh," "um," or "er"), and fewer hesitations ("I mean" or "you know"). They were less likely to hedge or qualify their statements ("maybe" or "sort of") and less likely to turn statements into questions ("That's how it happened, isn't it?" or "He was in the room, wasn't he?").

Part of that could just be due to the situation. After all, defendants are on trial, so they might try to be extra polite hoping they'll get off with a lesser sentence. Similarly, judges, lawyers, and expert witnesses have a lot more courtroom experience, so they're probably less nervous.

But while some of the variation was certainly driven by roles or experience, O'Barr wondered whether something more fundamental might be going on, whether beyond simply *reflecting* differences in who was talking, the language used might *impact* how speakers were perceived or the trial was resolved.

So with the help of some colleagues, he conducted an experiment.[2] They took a particular case, and a particular witness, and used actors to record two slightly different versions of the witness's testimony.

The facts stayed the same, but the language used to express those facts varied. In one version, the witness spoke like the professionals (judges, lawyers, and experts) did, and in the other, the witness spoke like ordinary people tend to.

For instance, when the lawyer asked, "Approximately how long did you stay there before the ambulance arrived?" the witness who talked like the professionals responded, "Twenty minutes. Long enough to help Mrs. Davis get straightened out." The witness who talked like an ordinary person said the same thing but hesitated along the way: "Oh, it seems like it was about, uh, twenty minutes. Just long enough to help my friend Mrs. Davis, you know, get straightened out."

Similarly, when the lawyer asked, "You know your way around?" the witness who spoke like the professionals just said "Yes," while the witness who spoke like ordinary people qualified things and said, "Yes, I guess I do."

Then, to test whether these differences had any impact, the researchers had different people listen to each recording and make judgments, like a member of a jury might. Listeners provided their thoughts about the witness and indicated whether the defendant in the case should pay the plaintiff damages, and if so, how much.

As O'Barr had predicted, slight differences in wording changed how the witness was perceived. Speaking like a professional made the witness seem more credible. Listeners saw them as more trustworthy, competent, and convincing, and were more likely to believe what they had to say.

And these changes also shaped listeners' reactions to the testimony. Even though the facts stayed the same, hearing a witness who talked like a professional made listeners think the plaintiff deserved thousands of dollars extra in damages.

O'Barr had uncovered the impact of speaking with power.

In the years since then, scientists have refined the exact components of "powerful" language. But at its core, the main idea remains the same. Speaking with power makes people seem confident. It makes them seem more certain, self-assured, and knowledgeable, which makes audiences more likely to listen and change their minds.[3]

Trump speaks with power, leadership gurus speak with power, and startup founders, at least the charismatic ones, speak with power. They lay out a vision, a worldview, a perspective, or an ideology that seems so convincing that it's hard to disagree. They seem so confident about what they are saying that it's hard to believe things could be any other way.

But speaking with power or confidence isn't something you're born with, it's something you can learn.

Four ways to speak with confidence are to: (1) ditch the hedges, (2) don't hesitate, (3) turn pasts into presents, and (4) know when to express doubt.

DITCH THE HEDGES

In 2004, researchers conducted an experiment about choosing a financial adviser.[4] Participants were told to imagine that they had inherited some money and were looking for an adviser to help them invest it. Some of their friends recommended Adviser A and others recommended Adviser B, so to help them decide, they were holding a competition. Each adviser would judge the probability that some individual stocks would increase in value after three months. Participants would check the adviser's judgments against the stocks' actual performance and hire the adviser whose judgments they preferred.

Adviser A, for example, said that there was a 76 percent chance that a particular company's stock would increase in value, and the stock ended up going up. Similarly, Adviser B said that there was a 93 percent chance that another company's stock would increase in value, and it went up as well.

After reading a few dozen predictions from each adviser, and viewing each stock's performance, participants were asked which of the two potential advisers they would hire.

In terms of accuracy, both advisers were equally good. Each was right 50 percent of the time and wrong the other 50 percent.

Unbeknownst to the participants, though, there was an important difference between the two advisers. Though they were equally accurate, one made judgments that were much more extreme. While their more moderate peer thought a stock had a 76 percent chance of going up, for example, the more extreme adviser thought it had a 93 percent chance. And while their more restrained counterpart thought a stock had an 18 percent chance of going down, the more extreme adviser thought it would be more like 3 percent.

One might think that people would prefer the moderate adviser. After all, they were better calibrated. Given all the uncertainty around performance, their more moderate estimates were more reasonable.

But that's not what happened.

In fact, when choosing advisers, almost three-quarters of people picked the more extreme one. They preferred guidance from someone who expressed greater confidence (seemed more certain), even though that confidence outstripped advisers' actual ability to estimate market trends.

And the reason is the same as what drives the power of powerful language. Whether choosing a money manager, listening to a witness, or picking a president, listeners are more persuaded when communicators seem more certain, or confident about what they are communicating.

Because when people speak with certainty, we're more likely to think they're right. Which candidate will do the best job? It's hard to know for sure, but if one speaks with certainty, it's harder to believe they could be wrong. After all, they just seem so confident.

The financial advisers conveyed their confidence through percentages. Their opinions might have been the same (the stock will go up), but they expressed those opinions with differing degrees of certainty. Compared to saying something has a 76 percent chance of happening, saying it has a 93 percent chance of happening makes it seem more likely, and makes the communicator seem more certain.

Words, though, can serve the same function. If someone says it will *definitely* rain, for example, it suggests there's a pretty good chance it will happen. Maybe not 100 percent but 95 percent or above. If someone says rain is *highly likely*, though, one might adjust the forecast down a bit. Closer to 95 percent rather than 100 percent.

Words like "probable" or "likely" suggest that the chance is lower (more like 70 percent), "about even" suggests around a 50 percent chance, and "unlikely" suggests the occurrence is even less likely. If someone says there's *almost no chance* of rain, you'd probably put the chance at almost zero.

Consequently, words like these not only convey predictions, they also shape action. If someone says it will *definitely* rain, for example, you might pack an umbrella; same if someone says that it's *clearly* going to rain or *absolutely* going to rain.

If someone says that it *might* rain, it *could* rain, or it is *unlikely* to rain, we're less likely to take the same precautions. We infer that there's a lower chance of getting wet, so we might leave the umbrella at home.

Just like the financial adviser study, though, words like these also shape how certain or confident communicators seem. If someone uses words like "definitely," "clearly," or "absolutely," it suggests a high degree of confidence. They're pretty certain about what's going to happen. It's going to rain, no question.

If they use words like "*might*" or "*could*," though, it signals more uncertainty. They think it could rain, but they're not really sure.

Words like "might" or "*could*" are called *hedges*. They're used to express ambiguity, caution, or indecisiveness. The same goes for words like "*guess*," "*speculate*," and "*assume*."

Examples of Hedges		
May/might	In my opinion	Kind of
Could	I think	Sort of
Seems/Seemed	It seems to me	Around
Probably	I believe	About
Maybe	I guess	Generally
Appears	I suppose	A bit

And hedges extend beyond expressions of likelihood. People can use hedges to express uncertainty about the exact amount of something ("I've had this for *around* three months"), uncertainty about what someone else said ("*According* to him, it works well"), and uncertainty about whether their opinions will generalize ("*In my opinion*, it's not worth the money"). When someone says "around," "arguably," "I believe," "generally," "kind of," "maybe," "presumably," "rarely," or "usually," they're hedging. They're expressing uncertainty in one way or another.

We hedge all the time. We note that we *think* something will work, that a solution *could* be effective, or that an alternate approach *might* work better. We suggest that something *seems* like a good course of action or that, *in our opinion*, something else is worth trying.

But without our realizing it, hedging can undermine our impact, because while we're sharing our thoughts or recommendations, by hedging, we're simultaneously undercutting them. We're suggesting that we're not sure those thoughts and recommendations are worth pursuing.

Indeed, when a colleague and I asked people how likely they were to follow someone else's advice, adding hedges to that advice made people less likely to go along. They were less likely to buy a recommended product or adopt a recommended course of action.

Because hedges can suggest a lack of confidence. Saying a solution *might* work, I *think* this is the best restaurant, or it's *probably* time to fix the engine all suggest someone is uncertain. They're uncertain about whether the solution will work, whether the restaurant is the best, or whether it's time to fix the car. And while being cautious can sometimes be a good thing, by making communicators seem less confident, hedges undermine their ability to influence others.

If someone's uncertain that a potential solution will work, why move ahead with it? If it's not clear that the restaurant is the best, maybe I'll just eat somewhere else. And if the mechanic isn't sure if it's time to fix the engine, not only will I skip the repair, maybe I'll find another mechanic who seems more knowledgeable.

That doesn't mean we should never hedge, but it certainly means that we should use hedges more deliberately.

Sometimes we hedge on purpose. We want to signal uncertainty, that we're not sure, or that an outcome is unclear. And if that's the goal, hedging can be great. But often we hedge without even realizing it. We're so used to qualifying statements that we toss in a hedge just because. And that's a mistake.

People often unconsciously preface things by saying "I think," "In my opinion," or "It seems to me." But while qualifying statements can be useful in some cases, they often make the subjectivity of what we're saying unnecessarily explicit.

When saying things like "She's a great hire" or "We should do this," it's already our opinion. After all, we're the one saying it. So unless we want to signal that it's subjective, prefacing the statement with "I think" or "In my opinion" limits our impact. It makes us seem less confident that others will draw the same conclusions, which makes others less likely to follow our lead.*

To convey confidence, then, ditch the hedges.†

And in their place, do what Donald Trump does instead. Use definites.

Words like "definitely," "clearly," and "obviously" remove any shred of doubt. Things are *unambiguous*, the evidence is *irrefutable*, and the answer is *undeniable*. *Everyone* knows it, it's *guaranteed*, and it's *precisely* what we need right now.

Definites do more than signal a lack of uncertainty. They suggest that things are 110 percent clear. The speaker is confident and the course of action is obvious. Making listeners more likely to follow them, and whatever they suggest doing.[5]

Examples of Definites		
Definitely	Guaranteed	Unambiguous
Clearly	Irrefutable	Unquestionable
Obviously	Absolutely	Essential
Undeniable	Everyone	Every time

---

* In cases where we do want to signal some uncertainty, use the right hedges. Rather than saying "It *seems* like this will work," for example, personalizing it by saying "It *seems to me* like this will work" actually increases persuasion because it conveys confidence. It says that you recognize that there is uncertainty, but you are admitting it.

† Where hedges happen also matters. Putting the hedge first ("*I think* this is the best"), for example, conveys more confidence than putting it after the statement ("This is the best, *I think*"). Putting the hedge first suggests that you are aware that something is your opinion, but you're pretty confident about that opinion. But hedging after the fact suggests backing away from the assertion, making both the information and the person communicating it seem less certain.

DON'T HESITATE

Hedging makes people seem less confident, less powerful, and less effective, but there's another linguistic choice that hurts even more, and that is hesitations.

Lindsey Samuels was trying to figure out how to improve her presentation style. The forty-one-year-old sales executive was making almost a dozen presentations a week. To existing clients, to prospective clients, and internally to colleagues and management.

But she wasn't having the impact she expected. Sometimes people took her advice, or went along with her suggestions, but too often they just kept doing what they were doing. Sticking with the status quo even though what she was suggesting was better.

She wanted to convert more prospects, convince more clients, and increase her impact, so we did a communications audit. Exploring what she was doing well, and what she might be able to do better.

I started by asking her to share a few of her presentation decks. Looking over them, though, it was hard to see any issues. The slides were clear, the language was concrete and concise, and she used great analogies to unpack complicated ideas. The slides themselves seemed strong.

If the content wasn't the issue, maybe it was the delivery. So I asked her if I could listen to her present the material. Covid-19 was in full swing, so rather than meeting in person we had online video calls.

From the first call, it was clear that something was off. The ideas themselves were well crafted, but something about the way she was presenting them was hurting their effectiveness. I just couldn't figure out what it was.

The conversations were recorded, so I tried going back and listening to them again. I'd listen to her voice over the different slides as she clicked through, but I still couldn't put my finger on what wasn't working.

Then, as part of its monthly software update, the video call company released some new features. Among better options for polling, and different ways of drawing on the screen, they added automatic transcription. Along with the video and audio recording of every meeting, a client would receive a written version of everything that had been said during the conversation.

I started sharing the transcripts with clients in case they were useful. Most people found them easier to skim than listen to the whole audio recording, but Lindsey in particular was horrified. "Do I really talk like that?" she asked. I told her I wasn't sure what she meant, and ten minutes later she shared a version of the transcript. Throughout the document, she had circled every time she had said "uh," "um," and "er." And there were a lot of them.

The transcript had highlighted the problem.

In the weeks that followed, Lindsey worked to cull the hesitations from her presentations. She practiced what she was going to say, scripted answers to questions in advance, and paused when necessary to get back on track.

And, it worked. She used fewer *um*s and *uh*s, and her pitches got sharper. In the next month, for example, she converted almost a third more potential prospects into clients. Cutting the fillers had made Lindsey a more effective communicator.

In regular, everyday speech, most of us say things like "uh," "um," and "er" a lot. It's a common verbal tic we use when we're collecting our thoughts or trying to sort out what to say next. And it's an easy crutch to lean on.

But while they're fine once in a while, when used too often, these hesitations or filler words can weaken whatever is being said.*

Imagine someone starts an important presentation by saying "I . . . um . . . think what I'm . . . uh . . . about to say . . . um . . . is really key." What would you infer about them and what they were going to talk about? Would they seem sharp and poised or anxious and underprepared? How confident would you be in their recommendation? Would you follow whatever they suggested?

Probably not. Indeed, research finds that hesitations are even more detrimental than hedges. They make people seem less powerful and authoritative and less effective at getting across whatever they are trying to communicate.[6]

When someone says "uh," "um," or "er" a lot, it suggests they don't know what they're talking about. That they're not really an expert.

In fact, whether people hesitate can be even more impactful than who that person was in the first place. In one study, students listened to tapes of speakers making opening comments at the beginning of a class.[7] The researcher was interested in how language shaped impression formation, so some students listened to a recording where the speaker hesitated a few times. They said "uh," "er," or "um" five to seven times throughout the message. For other students, the speaker didn't hesitate at all. Otherwise the content was the same.

Beyond what the speaker said, though, the study also manipulated how the speaker was described. Some students were told that the speaker was relatively high status (a professor), while others were told the speaker was lower status (a student teaching assistant).

When presenting ideas, we tend to think that status matters a lot. In

---

* Words such as "like," "you know," "I mean," "okay," and "so" often serve a similar function.

a meeting, for example, we think attendees will be more likely to listen if the boss says something rather than a subordinate. Or that the same idea will have more impact if a higher-status person brings it up.

And that's partially right. Status does matter. Sometimes. When students thought they were listening to a higher-status speaker, for example, they thought that person was a stronger, more dynamic presenter.

But what the speaker *said* mattered a lot more. Hesitating hurt. Speakers who hesitated were seen as less intelligent, less well informed, and less qualified. Listeners thought they had less expertise, and saw them as lower status, regardless of what their title actually was.

In fact, a "lower-status" speaker who didn't hesitate was perceived more positively than a "higher-status" speaker who did. Style trumped status.

So don't hesitate. One *uh* or *um* once in a while isn't the end of the world. It can signal we're thinking, or that we're not done with what we have to say.

But hesitating too often undermines our effectiveness. It makes us seem tentative or uncertain, and this lack of confidence hurts people's trust in us, and our opinions.*

Too often we use hesitations to fill conversational space. We start talking before we know what we want to say, so we have to toss in an *um* or *uh* at some point while we figure out what to say next. Indeed, that's why words like "um" and "uh" are often called *fillers*.

---

* So-called tag questions (e.g., "It's cold, isn't it?") have a similar effect. Turning a statement into a question suggests that someone is unsure of their opinion, and makes them less persuasive.

But waiting before talking can reduce the need for hesitations. It gives us time to figure out what to say and come across as more competent.

And pausing has other benefits as well. Studies my colleagues and I conducted found that pausing led speakers to be perceived more positively. It not only gave the audience time to process what was said, it encouraged them to respond with short verbal indicators of agreement (e.g., "Yeah," "Un-hunh," or "Okay"), which led them to like the speaker more overall.

So rather than saying "um" or "uh," take a second to pause. People will perceive us more positively and be more likely to follow our suggestions.

Overall then, the research on hedges and hesitations has clear implications. Giving a big presentation? Making an important sales pitch? Replace words, phrases, or actions that signal uncertainty with language that conveys conviction.

When someone says a solution is *obvious*, or the results are *unequivocal*, it exudes confidence. It suggests that rather than simply sharing an opinion, someone is sharing a truth about the world. And as a result, others are more likely to go along.

TURN PASTS INTO PRESENTS

Avoiding hedges and hesitations is one way to speak with confidence, but there's actually an even subtler approach.

People share their opinions all the time. They talk about products they love, movies they hated, vacations they enjoyed. Someone might say that a vacuum cleaner works well, a movie was boring to watch, or a beach had the best sunset.

When considering such information, we tend to focus on nouns, adjectives, and adverbs. We want to know whether a vacuum cleaner cleans well, a movie was interesting, or a vacation was worth going on.

Beyond nouns, adjectives, and adverbs, though, there's a feature that often receives little attention: verb tense.

Verbs are an indispensable part of communication. Nouns indicate what or who is being discussed, but verbs convey a noun's state or action. People walk. Emails are sent. Ideas are shared. Verbs help put the subject of an utterance into a particular position or motion. Without verbs, communication would just be meaningless finger-pointing at people, places, and things.

One way in which verbs vary is in their tense, or the time period they discuss. In English, verbs have a tense that describes *when* a particular action or event occurred. If someone says he "studied" for a test, for example, that indicates that the action occurred in the past; the studying happened previously.

The same action could also occur in the present. If someone says that she "is studying" for a test, it suggests that she is doing so now. By shifting the verb tense from past to present, a communicator indicates not only *what* he or she is talking about (studying) but *when* (past or present).

Verb tense communicates whether someone studies, is studying, or will study in the future. Similarly, it conveys whether a project is finished, is being finished, or will be finished at a later date.

Indeed, in many situations, tense is determined by the situation. If someone hasn't started studying yet, he can't say he "studied" (unless he's lying). Similarly, if a project is already done, a person won't usually put "will be" in front of the word "finished."

But in other situations, people can choose what verb tense to use. When talking about a job candidate, for example, someone can say that the candidate "seems" or "seemed" good. When describing a new vacuum cleaner, we can say that it "cleans" or "cleaned" well. And when describing a vacation destination, someone can say that the beaches "are" or "were" amazing.

My colleague Grant Packard and I wondered whether a shift in verb tense might influence persuasion, whether using present rather than past tense might make people more persuaded by something someone says.*

To test that possibility, we analyzed more than a million online reviews—hundreds of thousands of times in which people expressed opinions about products and services.

For each review, we quantified how often the reviewer talked about the past or the present and the impact of their review. Whether people found it helpful or useful and whether it made them more likely to buy whatever product or service was being talked about.

We started with books. Analyzing around a quarter of a million Amazon book reviews revealed that present tense increased impact. Saying a book "is" rather than "was" a good read or "has" rather than "had" great plot development led other people to find a review more helpful.

This was intriguing, but one could wonder whether it was due to something specific about the product category examined. Most people read a book only once, for example, so maybe book reviews tend to be in past tense and thus present tense is more unexpected.

So to test this possibility, we examined a category where the items are

---

* The English language doesn't have future-tense verbs—it adds an auxiliary verb such as "will" to an existing verb to communicate that something will be happening later—so we focused on the past and present tenses.

consumed multiple times: music. Most people listen to a song or album more than once, so present tense should be more likely to appear.

Even in music, though, we found the same result. Music reviews that used more present-tense verbs were more persuasive.

In fact, across a variety of different products (e.g., consumer electronics) and services (e.g., restaurants), the pattern persisted. Regardless of where we looked, present tense boosted impact. Saying music "is" rather than "was" great, a printer "does" rather than "did" a good job, or a restaurant "makes" rather than "made" delicious tacos led people to find the opinions more helpful, useful, and persuasive. Hearing that a beach "does" rather than "did" have great atmosphere, for example, made people think they would like that vacation destination more.

And the reason why is the same underlying reason behind the effect of hedges, hesitations, and powerful language.

Past tense suggests something was true at a particular point in time. If someone says, "That job applicant *was* sharp" or "The solution *worked* well," it suggests that the speaker thought the applicant was smart when they interviewed them yesterday or that the solution was effective when they implemented it last week.

Further, because personal experiences are naturally subjective, the use of the past tense suggests that what is being conveyed is subjective as well. Saying that a book *was* a fun read, for example, suggests that the opinion is based on a particular personal experience, that when the reviewer read the book, he or she enjoyed it.

Consequently, past tense can convey a degree of subjectivity and transience. This opinion is based on a particular person's experience, at a particular point in time.

Present tense, in contrast, suggests something more general and enduring. Saying something *works* well suggests not only that it *worked* well in the past, but that it continues to work well and will continue to do so in the *future*. Saying something *does* the job suggests not only that it *did* the job in the past but that it *will do* it again next time. Rather than a subjective opinion based on a particular person or experience, present tense suggests something more stable. Across people and time something is and will remain true. It's not just one person's past experience, others will have a similar experience in the future.*

Consequently, using the present tense increases impact because it changes how audiences see whatever was shared. Rather than a personal opinion based on limited experience, present tense suggests communicators are confident enough to make a general assertion about the state of the world. This isn't just how something was, it's how it is, and will be. It's not just my belief or judgment, it is an objective, universal truth.

And if something seems universal, it's probably going to have more impact. If a restaurant's food *was* good or a hotel *had* good service, maybe it's worth checking it out.

But if the food *is* good or the hotel *has* good service, it suggests those things are even better. Consequently, listeners are more persuaded to take a look.

Said another way, present tense suggests that speakers don't just have an opinion, they are relatively certain about it.

Telling patients a treatment *has* rather than *had* a 90 percent success rate or *lowers* rather than *lowered* cholesterol, should make them more willing to consider it. Saying a diet *helps*, rather than *helped*, people lose weight should make dieters more inclined to try it. And saying that a car

---

* This relates to the noun versus verb discussion in chapter 1. Rather than saying that someone *runs*, calling that person a *runner* suggests something more fundamental: that there is a degree of permanence or stability in the person's activity. The same goes for the present tense: compared to saying that something *was* good, saying that it *is* good suggests that the quality is inherent in the thing referenced.

is rather than *was* voted MotorTrend's Car of the Year should make consumers more interested in buying it.

Want to increase your influence? When presenting the results of a big project, talk about what you *find* rather than what you *found*. Talk about how people *are* doing something rather than how they *were* doing it. Even saying the food at a restaurant *is* rather than *was* excellent will make others more likely to go there.

Turning pasts into presents will make others more likely to listen to what we have to say.

KNOW WHEN TO EXPRESS DOUBT

So far, we've talked about a number of ways to convey confidence. Ditching hedges and hesitations, using definites, and turning pasts into presents. But while speaking with power can make us seem more certain and increase the chance people follow our suggestions, there are some situations where being more circumspect is actually more effective.

Thanksgiving is a special time. People come together from around the country to spend time with family and friends, eat delicious food, and give thanks for all the good things that happened in the past year.

But among the traditions, parades, and plates of turkey, recent Thanksgivings have come with a side of disagreement. Americans are more politically polarized than ever before, and while we're often surrounded by people we agree with, getting together with extended family often means stepping outside that bubble. Coming face-to-face with someone with whom you strongly disagree.

Many families post notices not to discuss politics, but inevitably someone brings it up. They've lost their job, are having trouble getting access to benefits, or are upset about the economy, and who they blame for those problems may be quite different from who we think is at fault. A polite conversation can quickly turn into a heated argument.

Rather than getting into a screaming match with crazy Uncle Louie in the living room, might there be a way to have a more civil discussion? And maybe even change the other person's mind a little?

A few years ago, researchers from Carnegie Mellon University recruited hundreds of people to discuss controversial topics,[8] polarizing subjects such as whether abortion should be legal, affirmative action should be used in college admissions, and undocumented immigrants who meet certain requirements should be able to remain in the country legally. Issues where different people have vastly different views.

Some participants were asked to write persuasive messages that would encourage other people to change their mind. In the case of abortion, for example, one pro-life advocate noted that various "factors can pressure a woman to have an abortion" and that "an abortion is probably one of the biggest decisions a person can make because it involves taking a life."

Other people were just asked to listen. After reporting their preexisting attitudes on the various issues (e.g., whether they were pro-choice or pro-life), they read a persuasive message that someone else had written and noted whether it changed their mind.

Importantly, before reading the persuasive appeal, some listeners read a short note in which the would-be persuader expressed doubt about their opinion. In it, the writer noted that while they believed they had thought carefully about the issue, they weren't completely convinced that they were right.

If certainty is always convincing, such an expression of doubt should reduce influence. After all, it's hard to be persuaded about something if the persuader isn't even sure they're right.

But in this context, it turned out that the exact opposite occurred. Expressing doubt about a contentious issue actually increased persuasion. Particularly among people who already had strong beliefs, hearing someone else wasn't sure about their opinion encouraged them to change their mind in that direction.

When trying to change the minds of people who disagree with us, we often think that it's best to be direct. We assume that if we just lay out the facts and provide unbiased information, the other side will come around to our way of thinking.

But not everyone sees "facts" the same way. Particularly when people feel strongly about something, motivated reasoning often encourages them to avoid or ignore information that threatens or challenges their beliefs.

Consequently, when trying to win over the other side, being too direct can backfire, leading the other person to become even more convinced of their initial opinion. Indeed, rather than being convincing, persuasive messages actually led a decent chunk of study participants to shift their opinions in the opposite direction.

In a sense, persuasion can be broken up into two stages. The second is where people consider someone else's views or the information provided and decide whether to update their beliefs. But before getting there, people must first decide how receptive to be. Whether or not they should listen in the first place.

People have an anti-persuasion radar or defense system that goes off when someone is trying to persuade them. The more something or

Curiosity

someone disagrees with them, the less likely they are to listen. Consequently, one reason change is so hard is that people are unwilling to even consider information that goes against their beliefs.

As a result, when dealing with opposing viewpoints, being a bit more indirect can often be more effective. Rather than starting with information, start by encouraging people to be more open minded and receptive.

This is why expressing doubt can help. Showing that we're conflicted or uncertain makes us seem less threatening. Expressing doubt about one's own view acknowledges that conflicting beliefs are valid, making the other side feel validated and more willing to listen. It recognizes that issues are complicated or nuanced, which increases receptiveness.

Uncertainty signals an openness to other perspectives.[9] So particularly when issues are contentious or people are dug in, expressing a little doubt can actually be more persuasive.

Popular press science coverage, for example, often treats research findings as more certain than they are. Front-page articles report that drinking coffee increases pancreatic cancer or that short bursts of exercise are more effective than longer ones. But while claims like these make for great headlines, they're often followed by pieces months or years later that report the exact opposite. Not only does this leave the public confused, but it reduces confidence in science itself.

While some argue that hedging will reduce the credibility of both scientists and journalists, this isn't the case. Reporting or acknowledging study limitations actually leads readers to see both scientists and journalists as more trustworthy.[10]

When people know something is uncertain, pretending it's not can backfire. It comes off as overconfident or unrealistic and undermines our ability to persuade.

So in situations like these, the best course of action can be to express doubt. Turning statements into questions, for example, is a great way to invite feedback. It shows that rather than being dogmatic, we're open to and actively soliciting others' views or participation in the process. Sure, we have an opinion, but we're also interested in listening to what others have to say.

The same goes for hedges and other tentative language. Words like "might," "could," and "possibly" are certainly a bit vague and ambiguous. Intelligence analysts, for example, are encouraged to steer clear of such terms in briefings because they can be misconstrued.

But while these words suggest something is uncertain, that uncertainty isn't always a bad thing. Particularly when we want to be careful and not go beyond what we know for sure. Saying that study results *suggest* rather than *demonstrate* that X causes Y, for example, indicates that a relationship might be there but is not 100 percent proven. As long as that's the goal, tentative language can actually be quite effective at communicating it.

Making Magic

Words do more than just convey facts and opinions. They signal how confident communicators are in the facts and opinions they are expressing. Consequently, words influence how we're perceived and the impact of what we say.

Want to be perceived more positively? Increase your impact?

1. **Ditch the hedges.** When the goal is to convey confidence, avoid words and phrases like "may," "could," and "in my opinion," which suggest that things, and the people saying them, are uncertain

2. **Use definites.** Rather than hedging, use definites instead. Words like "definitely," "clearly," and "obviously," which suggest whatever was said isn't just an opinion, it's an irrefutable truth.

3. **Don't hesitate.** *Um*s and *uh*s are natural parts of speech, but too many of them can undermine people's confidence in us and our message. So cut the fillers. To decrease hesitations, plan what to say in advance or pause to collect your thoughts when needed.

4. **Turn pasts into presents.** Using the present tense can communicate confidence and increase persuasion. So to signal certainty, rather than using past tense (e.g., "I *loved* that book"), use present tense (e.g., "I *love* that book") instead.

5. **Know when to express doubt.** While seeming to be certain is often beneficial, if we want to show we're open minded, receptive

to opposing viewpoints, or aware of nuances, expressing doubt can help.

By harnessing the language of confidence, we can signal our expertise, showcase our openness to opposing viewpoints, and encourage others to go along with what we're suggesting.

So far, we've talked about two types of magic words. Words that activate identity and agency, and words that convey confidence. Next, we'll talk about a third type of magic words, ones that help us ask the right questions.

3

Ask the Right Questions

When there's a difficult task at work that we can't seem to solve or a do-it-yourself project that proves tougher than expected, there are various ways to get unstuck. We can search online, brainstorm alternative approaches, or use trial and error, hoping to get it right.

There's a particular solution that we often tend to avoid, though, and that is asking for advice. We could ask a coworker, or call a friend and see if they can help, but we tend not to. We don't want to bother them, who knows if they'll be able to help anyway, and even if they can, we're worried that they'll think less of us. We think that asking for advice will make us seem incompetent, so we skip it all together.

Could that intuition be misguided?

———————

In 2015, a couple of my Wharton colleagues and a Harvard behavioral scientist asked people to complete sets of brain teasers.[1] They included easy questions like "Who was the first president of the United States?" (A: George Washington) and extremely difficult ones like "What is the correct definition of sesquipedalian?" (A: Tending to use long words).

Participants were told the scientists were interested in how communication shapes problem solving, and so each person would be matched with an anonymous partner to communicate with during the study. Each participant was told that they would complete some brain teasers first, and then their partner would complete the same brain teasers later in the experiment.

After completing the first set of brain teasers, the participants were told that they had done decently well (had gotten seven out of ten correct) but that their partner hadn't done quite as well (had gotten only six out of ten right). Then they received a note from their partner. For some, the note was just a simple greeting ("Hey there.") or a few words of solidarity ("Hey there. We're in this together."), but for others, a question was added at the end: "Hey there. Do you have any advice?"

In actuality, there was no "partner." The scientists were interested in how people are perceived when they ask for advice. Whether compared to just making chitchat, asking for advice would lead someone to be seen more positively or negatively. So they paired participants with a computer-simulated partner so they could see how what the "partner" said shaped how they were perceived.

After receiving the message from their "partner," participants rated them on a number of dimensions. How capable they thought their partner was, as well as how qualified and skilled.

If asking for advice makes people seem less competent, participants should have thought worse of partners who did so. Asking should have made them seem dependent on others or inferior.

But the opposite was true.

When the scientists analyzed the results, they found that asking for advice had made people think their partner was *more* competent, not less. And the reason why has everything to do with how asking someone for advice makes them feel.

People like feeling smart. They like feeling that other people think they're intelligent or have valuable things to say.

So asking for advice can make *us* look smart because it strokes the advice giver's ego. Rather than thinking we're not capable or are stupid for asking, advice givers draw a very different conclusion: "Of course my opinions are valuable, so this person is smart for asking for them."[*]

In some sense, asking for advice is almost like flattery. When we want people to like us, we often try to flatter them.

But while people like being flattered, they don't always trust the person flattering them. They're smart enough to realize that flattery comes with ulterior motives. Consequently, flattery can backfire.

Asking for advice is more effective, though, because it's less overt. Rather than telling someone they're great, asking them for advice *shows* that you hold them in high regard. That you think they're smart and value their opinion.

Consequently, not only does asking for advice gather valuable insights, it also makes the asker seem more competent. It makes advice givers feel smarter and more self-confident, which makes them see askers more positively as well.

---

[*] As with any strategy, there are boundary conditions: asking people for advice about something they know nothing about or about things that one should be able to solve oneself may backfire.

THE ADVANTAGES OF ASKING

Asking for advice is just one example of a much broader linguistic category: asking questions.

Whether at work or home, we're constantly asking (and answering) questions. Which solution do you like better? How much will it cost? Can you pick the kids up from practice? By some estimates, people ask (and answer) hundreds of questions a day.

Questions serve a variety of functions. Sure, they collect information or satisfy curiosity, but they also impact how the asker is perceived, the flow of conversation, and the social connection between the people talking.

In any social interaction, though, there are a seemingly infinite number of questions that could be asked. We could ask about someone's job, their interests, or even what they had for breakfast.

And while some questions seem like they might facilitate social connection, or make the asker look good, others seem less beneficial. Ask someone an embarrassing or intrusive question, for example, and they might not be as interested in talking to us again.

So are certain questions more effective than others? And how do we know the right types of questions to ask?

Four strategies for asking better questions are to: (1) follow up, (2) deflect difficulties, (3) avoid making assumptions, and (4) start safe, then build.

FOLLOW UP

When it comes to having successful interpersonal interactions, the age-old story is that it's all about personality and appearance. Some people are funnier, more charismatic, or more attractive than others, and these personal qualities just make them inherently more likable.

Another common explanation is that interpersonal similarity is key. It's often said that birds of a feather flock together, for example, and people with common interests may have more to talk about or better things to say.

But while these factors certainly play a role, they're somewhat disheartening. Because there's not much we can do to change them. Our height is fixed, it's tough to change one's personality, and while we can learn about blockchain, stoicism, or any other topic to try and fit in with a particular group of people, it's not the easiest thing to pull off.

Does that mean that the less attractive, less charming of us are doomed to fail? Or might there be another way?

To find out what drives first impressions, researchers from Stanford and UC Santa Barbara analyzed thousands of first dates.[2] They collected demographic information like age, physical characteristics like height and weight, and other features like hobbies and interests. In addition, they captured the interaction itself. Using microphones, they recorded what each person said throughout the date.

Not surprisingly, appearance played a role. Women, for example, were especially attracted to men who were taller than average. Similarity also mattered. People were more interested in going on a second date with another person who had similar interests and hobbies.

Even beyond these more fixed aspects, though, the words people used had a significant impact. Asking questions led to a better first impression. It made people feel like they clicked and made them more interested in going on a second date.[3]

Similar things have been found in a host of domains. In everyday getting-to-know-you conversations between strangers, for example, people who asked more questions were seen as more likable and fun to spend time with. And in doctor-patient interactions, patients were more satisfied when doctors asked them more questions about their lives and experiences.[4]

But when researchers looked further, they found that certain types of questions were more beneficial.

As the advice study suggests, asking questions can signal that we're interested in someone's viewpoint. That we care enough about them and their perspective that we want to learn more. Similarly, when going on a date or engaging in a regular everyday conversation, asking questions suggests that rather than just talking about ourselves, we're interested in our conversation partner and what they have to say.

Consequently, how beneficial different questions are depends in part on the degree to which they signal caring and interest.

Introductory questions, like "How are you?" are an automatic part of everyday discourse. As a result, it's hard to know whether someone is really interested or just being polite.

So-called mirror questions (ones that parrot back whatever comes in) have similar effects. When someone asks "What did you have for lunch?" we often respond with something like "A Reuben sandwich, how about you?" Compared to just answering the question ("A Reuben sandwich."), asking a question back suggests some interest. It indicates that rather than being completely self-focused, we're interested or aware enough to return the favor. But because volleying back the same question requires little effort, it's less likely to have interpersonal benefits. Similar to asking an introductory question, it's not clear whether we're actually interested or just being courteous.

Other types of questions can even be detrimental. If someone says,

"I'm taking a week off to go to the mountains," a response like "What's your favorite movie?" is a non sequitur. It has little relationship to what the first person said and doesn't follow what was being discussed. Rather than indicating caring and interest, it suggests the exact opposite: Someone either isn't listening or was so bored or uninterested that they went ahead and switched the topic. Not surprisingly, this doesn't lead the asker to be perceived positively and can even be worse than not asking any question at all.

Instead, a better type of question to ask is one that follows up on what was just said. If someone says they're a foodie, for example, asking them what types of food they like to eat. If someone says they're concerned a new project isn't working, asking them why they feel that way. And if someone says they can't wait for the weekend, asking them what they are looking forward to.

Follow-up questions encourage conversation partners to elaborate further. To say more, provide more detail, or give more texture.

And whether talking to friends or strangers, clients or colleagues, people who ask follow-up questions are perceived more positively. Indeed, when researchers analyzed dating conversations, they found that follow-up questions were particularly helpful in generating a positive impression. People who asked more follow-up questions were more likely to be asked on a second date.

Follow-ups work because they signal responsiveness. Rather than just being polite or asking questions to change the subject, follow-up questions demonstrate that someone listened, understood, and wants to know more.

Want someone to like you? Want to show that you listened and care? Don't just ask questions, ask the *right* questions.

Follow-up questions show we're dialed in. We're interested in the conversation, tracked what someone said, and are excited to learn more.

We value that person enough to listen to what he or she was saying and ask more about it.

DEFLECT DIFFICULTY

Follow-up questions are useful, but depending on the situation, other types of questions can be helpful as well.

Imagine interviewing for a job you're excited about. You're looking for a new challenge, and this opportunity seems like the perfect fit. Strong company, great position, and clear opportunities for advancement.

The interview gets off to a good start, and the interviewer seems to like you a lot, but then things hit a speed bump. After asking about your past experiences and the skills you'd bring to the role, the interviewer asks what you were paid in your previous position.

Difficult questions like this come up all the time. When negotiating, potential buyers are often asked how much they're willing to spend. When selling a car, potential sellers are often asked about the car's repair record. And when interviewing for a job, applicants are often asked why they left their last job, whether they have other offers, or even when they plan on having children.

Situations like these feel impossible. Not only are they uncomfortable, and in some cases illegal, but it often feels like there is no way out.

Our first instinct is to answer honestly. To respond direct and completely and tell the truth.

Doing so, however, is often costly. In negotiations, for example, someone who discloses private information may be exploited by their counterpart. Similarly, in job interviews, someone who tells the truth about their prior compensation, reason for leaving, or intent to have children may be offered less money or passed over for the position.

But while answering honestly often puts us at a disadvantage, the alternatives aren't much better.

Refusing to answer is also problematic. Not surprisingly, no one likes someone who declines to respond. Further, while we may decline to respond in an effort to keep sensitive information private, the lack of response often reveals more than we intended. If someone asks us why we left our last job, saying we'd prefer not to answer suggests there is negative information we're trying to cover up.

Lying is also far from ideal. We can try to omit relevant information, or tell an outright lie, but not only is deception dishonest, it has negative consequences if discovered.

In sum, when replying to direct, difficult questions it often feels like there are no good options.

A couple of my Wharton colleagues wondered whether there might be a better way to respond.[5] So in 2019, they recruited hundreds of adults and asked them to participate in an experiment on negotiations.

Participants were asked to imagine that they were the owner of an art gallery who was trying to sell a painting called *Hearts in the Spring*. They were told that they had purchased the painting for $7,000 and that it was part of a four-piece *Hearts* series by a particular artist.

They were also told that how much potential buyers would be willing to pay for the work would depend on whether the prospect already had other pieces in the series. Prospects who didn't have the other pieces in the series would only be willing to pay around $7,000, but those who'd already collected other pieces, and wanted to complete their set might be willing to pay twice as much. Each participant was then paired with another participant and negotiated the potential sale.

Different conversations evolved differently, but given its importance to the negotiation, participants inevitably asked the potential buyers if they had other paintings in the series. And this is where the key part of the experiment came in. To examine the impact of different responses to difficult questions, the researchers manipulated how the buyers (actually research assistants) responded to the direct question.

To some participants, the buyer responded honestly. They said that they did own other pieces in the *Hearts* collection, which suggested that they would be willing to pay more to buy the piece.

For other participants, however, the buyer declined to respond. Rather than answering the question, they said that they weren't prepared to discuss their collection at the moment.

Not surprisingly, while honesty worked well interpersonally, it was terrible from an economic standpoint. People liked the honest responders a lot, and said they trusted them, but also took all their money, extracting the highest possible price for the painting.

On the flip side, declining to respond worked well economically, but hurt interpersonally. While non-responders were able to get the painting for a lower price, their partners didn't trust them and thought they were twice as likely to be hiding something.

But the experimenters also tried a third strategy that was much more effective. Rather than providing the information, or declining to respond, another group of responders did something different: they deflected. Rather than disclosing that they owned another painting in the series, or saying that they didn't want to answer, they responded by asking something like "when were those other paintings made?" Or "are those for sale as well?"

They responded to a difficult question with a related question of their own.

It's hard to trust people who seem like they are hiding something. Consequently, explicitly declining to answer a question, even an unfair one, often has negative consequences.

But while hiding information is usually frowned upon, seeking information is not. In fact, just the opposite. Asking questions in a job interview, for example, can be a great way to show interest in the position or the company. Similarly, as shown in the *Advice* study, people love being asked for their opinion.

Consequently, responding with a relevant question flips the script. Rather than seeming evasive, it seems interested and engaged. Rather than making us look disagreeable and untrustworthy, it makes us look like we care and want to learn more.

And questions do all this while deflecting attention. Because beyond just seeming evasive, the bigger problem with declining to respond is that it doesn't change the conversation's focus. The question asker is still looking for the answer, and if anything, declining makes the missing answer seem even more important. When a defendant evokes their Fifth Amendment right against self-incrimination, it just makes them seem even more guilty.

Questions, though, are like spotlights: They shine attention on a particular topic or piece of information. So by responding to a difficult question with a relevant question of our own, we move the spotlight away from us and on to something else.

If an interviewer asks a job applicant when she is planning on having kids, responding with "Do you have any kids?" redirects the conversation. It shifts the focus away from her and onto the personal life of the interviewer.

If the interviewer has kids, the conversation can move to talking about them (which will probably make the interviewer feel warmly), and if they don't, the two can commiserate about how much work kids are. All the while allowing the interviewee to refrain from having to answer the initial, unfairly prying question.

Indeed, the researchers found that deflection was the best way to respond to difficult direct questions. It enabled participants to get a better deal in the negotiation (getting the painting at a lower price) than honest disclosure, while also being viewed as more trustworthy and likable than declining to disclose.

Deflecting works in a host of difficult situations. In negotiations, for example, when asked what the highest amount is that we're willing to pay, we can respond by asking "Is there a number you had in mind?" Or when asked in an interview what the salary of our last position was, we can respond by asking "Can you share a bit more detail about the salary range for this position?"

Deflecting even works when, rather than keeping information private, we're just trying to protect the question asker's feelings. When someone asks if a presentation went well, or a piece of clothing looks good on them, and the answer is no, deflection can help us soften the blow. Questions things like "How do you think it went?" or "Interesting, where can I buy something like it?" avoids unnecessarily negative feedback and allows us to sort out whether it's worth telling them nicely or just leaving well enough alone.

As with many strategies we've discussed, though, it's important to apply deflection the right way. Deflection is not just about responding to one question with another. To work, deflection requires sticking close to the topic at hand. If an interviewer asks about the salary at our last job, for example, asking them what they had for breakfast just seems evasive. Like we're dodging the question.

The key is asking a related question that shows interest. Signaling that we are seeking relevant information rather than hiding it.

AVOID ASSUMPTIONS

Deflection is helpful when someone asks us a tough question, but asking the right questions also impacts our ability to uncover the truth.

We're often trying to collect information from others. We want to know the positives and negatives about a neighborhood, the good and bad news about a used car, or what a job candidate's strengths and weaknesses might be.

Unfortunately, other people's incentives aren't always aligned with ours. Realtors, for example, have an incentive to talk about great school systems and walkable streets but omit the stifling property taxes and restrictive zoning laws. Used-car sellers have an incentive to highlight the things that were recently repaired and neglect to mention the things that weren't. And job candidates have an incentive to talk about a recent promotion (because it increases the chance that they will be hired) but not the time they were fired for spending company time on social media (because it won't).

How can we encourage people to divulge negative information, even when it might put them at a disadvantage?

The simplest answer would seem to be to ask. To ask the job candidate whether they had ever been fired or the realtor if the neighborhood
has any downsides. But it turns out that *how* we ask such sensitive questions has a big impact on whether we actually uncover the truth.

To examine the right way to ask sensitive questions, some researchers
invited a couple hundred people to negotiate the sale of a used iPod.[6]
They were told to imagine that they had received the iPod as a birthday
gift, and loved it, but they had decided to buy an iPhone, and given it
had all the same features and more, they didn't need the iPod anymore.

Fortunately, the iPod was in great condition. It had been kept in a
plastic case to avoid being banged or scratched and, as a result, looked
as good as new. It also had a bunch of music already on it that the buyer
could either keep or dispose of.

The only issue was two instances when the iPod had completely fro-
zen. Fixing that had involved resetting all the factory defaults, which
had deleted all the music that was stored on the device. A couple hours
had been wasted each time that had happened, and there was no telling
if and when it might happen again.

Each participant engaged in a brief online negotiation with a potential buyer. In addition to mentioning some general things, the potential buyer asked a question. For some participants, the question
was a general one ("What can you tell me about the iPod?"). For others, a more direct question was asked. Specifically, whether the iPod
had had any issues in the past ("The iPod doesn't have any problems,
does it?").

Not surprisingly, sellers tended to focus on the positives. They talked
about how much memory the iPod had, how it was in great shape, and
how it even came with a protective case. As in most strategic information
exchanges, they emphasized the aspects that benefited them.

In fact, when asked the general question of "what can you tell me about it?" only 8 percent of sellers volunteered that there had been any issues with the iPod freezing in the past. Even though the same thing might happen again in the future, almost no one volunteered the negative information because they knew it would hurt how much they would get for the device.

Just asking questions, by itself, clearly wasn't enough. So did directly asking about the problems help?

Kind of.

If buyers directly asked about any potential issues ("The iPod doesn't have any problems, does it?"), some sellers were relatively forthcoming. Around 60 percent of them fessed up and noted that the iPod had a history of crashing.

But while asking directly encouraged some sellers to divulge the negative information, four out of ten still avoided answering it to create a more positive impression, which means buyers ended up overpaying for the device almost 40 percent of the time.

This is a bit disconcerting. After all, even when asked what seemed like the most direct question possible, the sellers still didn't provide a straight answer.

Maybe some people are just dishonest. Whatever question they were asked, they could find a way to weasel out of answering it. Liars are liars, and there's nothing to be done.

But while that may be true, another problem was the language itself. Because while a question like "It doesn't have any problems, does it?" asks about the presence of problems, it also makes an implicit assumption. That there aren't any.

As the research on speed dating and asking for advice suggests, questions shape how we're perceived. But they not only shape how smart or likable we seem, they shape the inferences others make about our knowledge and intentions.

Asking something like "What can you tell me about the iPod?" makes it easy for respondents to focus on the positive. After all, it wasn't a direct question about problems, so there's no reason to bring them up.

Even a more direct question ("It doesn't have any problems, does it?") suggests that the buyer doesn't have any real information about potential problems or reason to believe that there might be any. So for the seller, omitting those issues still feels safe. Sure, it's dishonest, but if there are incentives to be overly positive and little chance of getting caught, the downside seems low.

So are we just stuck with people lying to us 40 percent of the time?

Not quite. Because a third type of question greatly increased the likelihood of a more informative response.

Even without realizing it, questions like "It doesn't have any problems, does it?" presume that there aren't any issues. While they do directly ask about problems, they simultaneously communicate the questioners' assumption that no problems exist.

Compared to a general question ("What can you tell me about it?"), such questions signal that the question asker is aware that there could be issues, but also that they aren't super interested in investigating them. Either because they assume that such issues don't exist, or that they are averse to confrontation, and thus unlikely to pursue an assertive line of questioning.

But another way to ask about potential problems is to flip the assumption. To presume that problems exist rather than don't.

Questions like "What problems does it have?" do exactly that. Rather than implicitly assuming no issues, they assume there are some and want to root them out.

Further, such negative assumption questions signal something different about the question asker. Rather than not being aware of issues, or wanting to avoid them, negative assumption questions signal the asker both knows there could be issues and is assertive enough to ask about them.

Which makes it much harder to respond evasively. Indeed, when a third set of potential buyers asked "What problems does it have?," potential sellers were much more forthcoming. Even though positive and negative assumption questions both directly asked about problems, negative assumption questions led sellers to be 50 percent more likely to fess up that problems could exist.*

Questions not only solicit information, they reveal it. They reveal information about our knowledge, our assumptions, and even how assertive we're going to be.

Consequently, the questions we ask not only shape how we are perceived but the truthfulness of the answers we receive. Sure, some subset of people might lie regardless or do their best to be evasive, but they're much less likely to do so when they feel like someone else might catch them.

And the importance of asking these types of questions goes far beyond warding against lying.

Doctors see back-to-back patients all day. They're pressed for time and have to move quickly, so they ask questions that help them do that. "You don't smoke, right?" they might say to someone in for her yearly

---

* One could wonder whether there might be an interpersonal penalty for asking such an assertive question. Maybe it will garner the desired information, but it makes the person who asks it look bad: pushy, annoying, or too aggressive. But that doesn't seem to be the case. In fact, individuals who asked such questions weren't perceived any less positively than others.

exam, or "You're getting enough exercise, right?" Questions like these help them churn through patients at a fast clip.

But by asking questions that presume the lack of an issue, they're unintentionally encouraging a particular type of response. If a patient has been smoking or not exercising as much as they should, are they really going to contradict the doctor? After all, the doctor has made it so easy to just say "No" or "Yes" that the path of least resistance is pretending that there aren't any problems.

The more aversion there is to revealing certain information, the more important it becomes to ask questions that avoid making (positive) assumptions. Avoid presuming the absence of an issue. People know that the doctor will frown on smoking or lack of exercise, so they'll use any excuse to avoid bringing such information up. If they've been abusing alcohol or drugs, the reticence to bring it up will be even higher.

The same goes when trying to get audiences to speak up. When making presentations or teaching complicated ideas, people often say things like "You don't have any questions, do you?" But swapping that out for "What questions do you have?" will encourage more people to follow up if they don't understand.

In sum, while there are always incentives to selectively report information, asking the right questions can help us get to the bottom of things. To uncover whatever negatives might be there and incorporate them in our decision making.

But it's not enough just to be direct. We have to be direct in a way that not only shows that we're aware that there could be negative information, but that we are assertive enough to keep looking for it until we find it.

Sure, a landlord isn't motivated to reveal that the neighbors have wild parties, rowdy kids, and a barking dog. But asking a question like "How are the neighbors?" won't encourage them to reveal that information. Instead, we have to phrase questions the right way (e.g., have residents ever complained about the neighbors in the past?). Avoid (positive) assumptions, and we're much more likely to get a straight answer.

START SAFE, THEN BUILD

Knowing the right questions to ask is a valuable skill. Rather than any question being equally good, some ways of asking are more effective than others.

But beyond *which* questions to ask, certain types of questions can be better to ask at different times in a conversation.

In the late 1960s, University of California, Berkeley, graduate student Arthur Aron was trying to figure out what to study. He was doing a master's degree in social psychology and was looking for something that hadn't already been investigated in too much depth. Something people didn't think could be studied scientifically, but that he could figure out a way to crack.

While trying to sort that out, he was also dating a fellow student, Elaine Spaulding. They fell in love, and when they kissed, he realized two things. First, this was the person he wanted to spend the rest of his life with, and second, love might just be the right topic for him to study.

More than fifty years later, Arthur and Elaine are still together. And they've done some incredible things. They've traveled the world, written bestselling books, and lived everywhere from Paris and Toronto to Vancouver and New York.

But along the way, the Arons also changed the way we think about interpersonal relationships. From friendships and romantic partners to strangers who are meeting for the first time.

Their research examines how people form and maintain connections, and the role such bonds play in personal growth and development. They've studied how doing novel or exciting things with a partner improves your relationship, how cross-group friendships can reduce prejudice, and the neural mechanisms underlying the euphoria of intense romantic love (hint, they're the same ones that respond to cocaine).

Some of the research they are probably most famous for, though, is work on how to bring people together. Strong relationships are vital. Social connections not only give us someone to talk to, they help us live happier, healthier lives. Relationship quality is a bigger predictor of happiness than wealth or success, and it's a huge predictor of health. Dozens of studies find that people who have strong social support from their family, friends, or community have lower rates of anxiety and depression, higher self-esteem, and longer lives.

But while the benefits of interpersonal closeness are clear, such relationships usually take a while to blossom. It often takes multiple interactions before colleagues become friends, and numerous dates over weeks and months to start building a strong romantic relationship.

Further, developing stronger relationships can be challenging. Say you wanted to become friends with someone at the office, for example, or deepen a relationship with an acquaintance. You can try to bump into them, or find an excuse to ask them to grab a cup of coffee, but it's often hard knowing exactly what to say.

The Arons wondered whether there might be a more effective way. A step-by-step foolproof process that would make any two people feel closer. A technique that friends, would-be romantic partners, and even strangers who just met could follow and, in less than an hour, reap the benefits.

This sounds difficult. Impossible even. After all, trust and intimacy aren't built overnight.

And yet, sometimes, in the face of all odds, social connections form and flourish. Strangers happen to sit next to one another on a flight, and by the time they get off the plane, they're the best of friends. Colleagues who didn't know, or even didn't like, each other before happen to be paired up for a team-building event and are inseparable thereafter.

In the late 1990s, the Arons built and tested an approach to encourage the formation and strengthening of social bonds. A technique to create closeness with anyone, anytime, anywhere.

And this approach, at its core, relies on asking the right questions.

Two people are asked to read, and discuss, three sets of questions. The first set starts simply enough: "Given the choice of anyone in the world, whom would you want as a dinner guest?" One partner answers the question, and then the other does the same.

Then, they move on to the next question: "Would you like to be famous? In what way?" Each takes a turn answering, and then they move on to the third question: "Before making a telephone call, do you ever rehearse what you are going to say? Why?"

Partners take turns reading questions and answering them, and they're given fifteen minutes to complete as many of the first set of questions as they happen to get to.

FIRST SET OF QUESTIONS

---

1. Given the choice of anyone in the world, whom would you want as a dinner guest?

2. Would you like to be famous? In what way?

3. Before making a telephone call, do you ever rehearse what you are
    going to say? Why?

4. What would constitute a "perfect" day for you?

5. When did you last sing to yourself? To someone else?

6. If you were able to live to the age of 90 and retain either the mind
    or body of a 30-year-old for the last 60 years of your life, which
    would you want?

7. Do you have a secret hunch about how you will die?

8. Name three things you and your partner appear to have in common.

9. For what in your life do you feel most grateful?

10. If you could change anything about the way you were raised, what
    would it be?

11. Take four minutes and tell your partner your life story in as much
    detail as possible.

12. If you could wake up tomorrow having gained any one quality or
    ability, what would it be?

Once fifteen minutes are up, the partners move on to the second set
of questions. As before, partners take turns reading the questions and
answering them and complete as many of the questions as they can or
want to in fifteen minutes.

SECOND SET OF QUESTIONS

1. If a crystal ball could tell you the truth about yourself, your life,
    the future, or anything else, what would you want to know?

2. Is there something that you've dreamed of doing for a long time?
    Why haven't you done it?

3. What is the greatest accomplishment of your life?

4. What do you value most in a friendship?

5. What is your most treasured memory?

6. What is your most terrible memory?

7. If you knew that in one year you would die suddenly, would you change anything about the way you are now living? Why?

8. What does friendship mean to you?

9. What roles do love and affection play in your life?

10. Alternate sharing something you consider a positive characteristic of your partner. Share a total of five items.

11. How close and warm is your family? Do you feel your childhood was happier than most other people's?

12. How do you feel about your relationship with your mother?

After fifteen minutes have elapsed, they go to the last set of questions.

LAST SET OF QUESTIONS

1. Make three true "we" statements each. For instance, "We are both in this room feeling . . ."

2. Complete this sentence: "I wish I had someone with whom I could share . . ."

3. If you were going to become a close friend with your partner, please share what would be important for him or her to know.

4. Tell your partner what you like about them; be very honest this time, saying things that you might not say to someone you've just met.

5. Share with your partner an embarrassing moment in your life.

6. When did you last cry in front of another person? By yourself?

7. Tell your partner something that you like about them already.

8. What, if anything, is too serious to be joked about?

9. If you were to die this evening with no opportunity to communicate with anyone, what would you most regret not having told someone? Why haven't you told them yet?

10. Your house, containing everything you own, catches fire. After saving your loved ones and pets, you have time to safely make a final dash to save any one item. What would it be? Why?

11. Of all the people in your family, whose death would you find most disturbing? Why?

12. Share a personal problem and ask your partner's advice on how he or she might handle it. Also, ask your partner to reflect back to you how you seem to be feeling about the problem you have chosen.

The Arons conducted experiments to see whether the approach worked.[7] They asked hundreds of strangers to have short conversations, some of whom followed the structure of the thirty-six questions. Then, at the end of their interaction, the strangers reported how close and connected they felt to their conversation partner.

Just a single forty-five-minute interaction between two people who had previously been strangers. Nowhere near the weeks and months it usually takes to form social bonds.

And yet, this interaction, built solely on questions, had a huge impact. Compared to partners who just engaged in small talk, those who went through the intervention felt closer and more connected. Relative to their other relationships, including with friends, family members, and everyone else, they reported feeling like their partner, a person they had only just met, fell somewhere in the middle in terms of closeness.

Further, the approach worked equally well regardless of whether people were similar or different at the outset. Even between partners with different values and preferences or different political leanings, the questions helped make them feel closer and more connected.

Since then, this so-called Fast Friends technique has helped create emotional bonds between thousands of strangers. Art uses them regularly in his lectures and freshman classes to help people connect. People have applied them to help facilitate cross-race friendships and reduce prejudice.[8] They've even been used to bolster trust and improve understanding between police officers and community members in cities where tensions are running high.

But just as interesting as their utility is why these questions are so useful in the first place. Would any questions be equally connecting? And if not, what is it about these questions, in this order, that is so impactful?

The first answer is easy. No, not all questions are equally connecting. Strangers who engaged in normal, undirected small talk instead also asked and answered questions (e.g., "How did you celebrate last Halloween?" or "What did you do this summer?"), but they didn't boost closeness to the same degree.

Developing close relationships often involves self-disclosure. Eventual friends or partners don't start close. They start by exchanging pleasantries, making chitchat, and filling conversational space.

But what often separates relationships that evolve into something more is the ability to move past that. To go beyond the small talk and get to something deeper. To reveal things about oneself, learn things about someone else, and truly connect.

And questions can help. Not just any questions, but deep, probing ones like "If you were to die this evening with no opportunity to communicate with anyone, what would you most regret not having told someone? Why haven't you told them yet?"

This isn't your run-of-the-mill "How are you?" or polite inquiry about what someone is doing this weekend. These are tough, thought-provoking questions that encourage people to think, reflect, and generate a thoughtful answer.

Questions like these encourage people to open up. Rather than musing about the weather, or some other superficial topic, these questions delve deeper. They foster self-disclosure and self-revelation and encourage people to express something about who they really are.

One intuitive solution, then, would be to skip the small talk. Forget the chitchat and jump to these deep, probing questions right away.

But here's the problem. Imagine that a stranger you just met two minutes ago asked you what you would most regret not having told someone if you died. How would you respond? Would you happily answer the question, honestly revealing things about yourself even though you just met them?

Probably not.

In fact, we'd probably find an excuse to get out of the conversation. Or if we did answer, we'd give a pretty surface response. Because we wouldn't feel comfortable enough yet to actually be honest. We wouldn't feel like we know them well enough to be willing to share. Generating true, deep, self-disclosure requires some sort of existing social connection.

And therein lies the challenge. Deep self-disclosure requires social connection. But to get to that social connection, people need to have disclosed things about themselves previously.

This catch-22 is part of the reason why the Fast Friends procedure is so effective. Rather than jumping to the heavy stuff right away, it eases people in, encouraging gradual self-disclosure.

The initial questions are innocuous enough; broad, easy, softballs, lobbed over to break the ice. Who you'd want as a dinner guest is a fun question that anyone can answer. It doesn't feel too private or personal, so people are comfortable sharing their responses even with strangers they've just met.

But while the question feels safe enough to answer, the answers begin to provide a window, however small, into who someone is. If your partner picks LeBron James, the pope, Albert Einstein, or Martin Luther King, Jr., it gives you some sense of who they are and what they value. They love sports, value religion, are into science, or care about social justice. It doesn't tell you everything, but it starts to build a base.

And that tiniest bit of self-disclosure, that microrevelation, provides the fuel that encourages their partner to do the same. To reveal a bit about themselves in response. This, in turn, encourages more self-disclosure from the other side, and the connection builds from there.

Mutual vulnerability fosters closeness, but getting to the point where two people are willing to be vulnerable with each other is tough. Everyone is worried about putting themselves out there, saying too much, or not having their efforts reciprocated. Many people are willing to go second, but few are willing to be first.

The Fast Friends questions help. They don't start too big, but they also don't stay too small. They start safe and they build, becoming increasingly probing and revealing. And by requiring both parties to respond, they ensure everyone is contributing, deepening trust. The sustained, escalating, and reciprocal self-disclosure strengthens interconnectedness and can bring any two people closer together.

Making Magic

It's often been said that there are no stupid questions. But there are certainly better and worse ones.

Questions help us collect information, but they also communicate things about us, direct the flow of conversations, and build social bonds. Consequently, we need to understand which questions to ask and when to ask them.

Here are five guidelines to consider:

1. **Ask for advice.** Not only does it garner useful insights, it makes us seem smarter as well.

2. **Follow up.** Asking questions makes us look good, and facilitates positive interactions, but follow-up questions are particularly useful because they show we're interested and care enough to learn more.

3. **Deflect difficulty.** When someone asks an unfair question, asking a related one back allows us to direct the conversation in a different direction, showing interest while keeping personal information private.

4. **Avoid assumptions.** When trying to get people to divulge potentially negative information, be careful of questions that assume things away.

5. **Start safe, then build.** Deep self-disclosure requires social connection. But to get to that point, people need to feel safe first.

So to deepen social relationships, or turn strangers into friends, start simple and build from there, encouraging reciprocal self-disclosure.

Knowing what to ask, and when, can help us make better impressions, collect useful information, and foster more meaningful connections with those around us.

Beyond questions, though, there's another type of magic word that deserves attention, and that is the language of concreteness.

4

Leverage Concreteness

A few years ago, I was on the way to the airport when I got the text every traveler dreads: my flight had been canceled. I'd been on the road for a couple days, and was looking forward to getting home, so this was less than ideal. Further, I'd picked this flight so I could make it home in time to put the kids to bed, and now rather than being there, or at least spending more time with the consulting client I'd come to visit, I'd be stuck at the airport.

To make matters worse, the airline had tried to rebook me, but rather than a direct flight later that day, I'd been rebooked on a connecting flight the next one. Now I was really pissed, so I called customer service to try to fix things.

The agent on the other end of the line was less than helpful. Rather than actually listening, or trying to really understand the problems, they kept walking through what felt like a script. Using stock phrase after stock phrase in an attempt to show they "cared" rather than putting in the work of actually caring. After twenty minutes of back-and-forth, I was able to get onto a waiting list for a direct flight later that evening, but by then I was pretty furious.

The kind Uber driver who'd been forced to listen to the conversation offered his condolences, and we ended up striking up a conversation. I mentioned how frustrated I was but also how bad I felt for the customer service representatives who had to deal with everyone's problems. It wasn't their fault that the flight had been canceled, yet there they were, fending off angry people like me all day long, one after the other.

It seemed to me like a tough job, but the Uber driver said it was quite the contrary. He mentioned that his daughter worked in customer service for one of the airlines and loved it. In fact, she was so good at making customers happy that the airline had promoted her to teach other agents how to be more effective.

At first, I was surprised. Making customers happy in this context seemed quite difficult. Most callers are dealing with canceled flights, delays, or lost bags and it wasn't like the agent could snap their fingers and magically make the problems go away.

But as I thought about it more, I started to wonder: If his daughter was so good at dealing with difficult situations, what was she saying that helped patch things up? Beyond what agents could offer (e.g., a credit or alternate flight), might there be certain ways of communicating that make customers more satisfied?

To study that question, Grant Packard and I assembled a data set of hundreds of customer service calls to a big online retailer[1]: someone from Arkansas whose luggage wouldn't unlock; someone from St. Louis whose shoes were defective; and someone from Sacramento who needed help returning a shirt that didn't fit.

With the help of a transcription company and a team of research assistants, we turned the recordings into data. We transcribed the calls, separated out what the agent and customer had said, and even measured vocal features such as pitch and tone.

Each customer called for a different reason, but many calls followed a familiar script. The agent introduced themselves, the customer outlined whatever issue they were having, and the agent tried to solve it. Attempting to sort out why the luggage wouldn't unlock, figuring out what was wrong with the shoes, or helping the customer return the shirt. The agent would look in their system, or chat with a manager, and collect whatever information was needed. Then, after hopefully resolving the issue, they'd explain what they'd found or done, see if the customer had any more questions, and say goodbye.

But while the calls themselves had a similar structure, the outcomes were quite different. Some customers were happy with the service and found the agent quite helpful. Others, not so much.

Not surprisingly, part of this was driven by what customers were calling about. Some called about problems with their accounts, and others called about trouble with an order. Some called about bigger issues and others called about smaller ones.

But even controlling for what people called about, customer demographics, and dozens of other factors, how agents talked played an important role. A certain way of speaking boosted customer satisfaction.

And to understand that way of speaking, we have to understand a fourth type of magic words: what's known as linguistic concreteness. Three ways to apply it are to: (1) make people feel heard, (2) make the abstract concrete, and (3) know when it's better to be abstract.

HOW TO MAKE PEOPLE FEEL HEARD

Some things are quite concrete. Doors, tables, chairs, and cars are all specific, tangible, physical objects. You can see them with your eyes and touch them with your hands. You have a clear sense of what they are and can even picture them in your mind. If asked to draw what a table looks like, for example, even a five-year-old can do it.

Other things, however, are less concrete. Take love, for example, freedom, or ideas. All these are intangible concepts that are tougher to grasp. They're not physical objects, so we can't touch them, and it's harder to picture them in our minds. Ask someone to draw democracy, for example, and you'd probably get a blank stare. It's not clear what democracy looks like, if it looks like anything at all.

Beyond some things being naturally more concrete than others, though, in many situations the same thing can be talked about in more or less concrete ways.

Denim leg coverings, for example, can be described as *pants* or *jeans*. Pie can be described as *really* good or *mouthwateringly* good. And rather than calling something a "digital transformation," it can be described as "enabling customers to buy things online as well as in the store." In all cases, the latter version (jeans or mouthwateringly good) is more concrete. It's more specific, vivid, and easier to picture or imagine.

The same goes for the customer service calls we examined. A service representative answering a request to find a pair of shoes, for example, could say that they would go look for *them, those shoes,* or *those lime green Nikes.* Someone responding to an inquiry about a delivery could say the package will be arriving *there,* at your *place,* or at your *door.* And someone discussing a refund could say, we'll send you *something,* a *refund,* or your *money.*

Again, in all three examples, the latter versions use more concrete language. *Those lime green Nikes* is more concrete than *them*, *at your door* is more concrete than *there*, and *your money back* is more concrete than *refund*, which is more concrete than *something*. The words used are more specific, tangible, and real.

These variations might seem like simple turns of phrase, but they had an important impact on how customers felt about the interaction.

Using concrete language significantly increased customer satisfaction. When customer service agents used more concrete language, customers were more satisfied with the interaction and thought the agent had been more helpful.

And the benefits of linguistic concreteness extended beyond how customers felt. When we analyzed almost a thousand email interactions from a different retailer, we found similar effects on purchase behavior. When employees used more concrete language, customers spent 30 percent more with the retailer in the following weeks.

Talk may seem cheap, but this time it more than paid off.

Whether solving problems, or selling products and services, frontline employees deal with dozens of customers a day. Call center representatives go from one call to the next, helping one customer with a faulty suitcase and another with a website login issue. Retail employees go from helping one person find a jacket to helping someone else return a pair of pants. And salespeople often go from one pitch meeting to the next, touting benefits to various clients.

In situations like these, it's easy to fall back on a set of stock phrases. "I'd be happy to help with that" or "Sorry about the issue" whether the *that* or *the issue* in question is a jacket, pants, or anything else. Such abstract, generic responses help save time and effort because they're applicable to almost any situation.

But that wide applicability has a downside.

Imagine shopping for clothes. You find a T-shirt you like but can't find the gray color you're looking for, so you ask two employees for help. One employee says, "I'll go look for that," and the other says, "I'll go search for that T-shirt in gray." If you had to pick one, which employee would you say did a better job of listening to what you said?

When we asked hundreds of people questions like this, the latter, more concrete response ("I'll go search for that T-shirt in gray.") won by a landslide. Generic responses (e.g., "I'll go look for that.") can be used in any situation, but this generality means they're not very specific or concrete. And consequently, it's less clear the person speaking abstractly actually *listened*.

Because people, whether customers or otherwise, want to feel heard. When someone calls customer service, asks to speak to a manager, or comes into your office with something on their mind, they want to feel like someone is listening to their concerns and going to address them.

But for someone to feel heard, three things have to happen. First, they have to feel like the other person *paid attention* to what they said. Second, they have to feel like the other person *understood* what they said. And third, the other person has to *demonstrate that they listened*.

This last part is key. Imagine talking to someone who provided no response. They might have attended to everything we said. They might even have understood it completely. But without some sort of outward signal that indicates they listened, it's impossible to know whether or not they actually did.

Consequently, it's not enough just to listen. To make people feel heard, we have to *show* them that we listened. We have to respond in a way that demonstrates that we attended to and understood what they said.

And this is why concrete language is so valuable. A customer service representative may have paid attention, and understood the problem, but without some outward signal of understanding, there is no way for the customer to know.

Concrete language provides that signal. Using specific, concrete language shows that rather than just going through the motions, someone went to the effort to attend to and understand what was said. Or, said differently, to listen.

Concrete language boosted customer satisfaction, and purchase, because it showed customers that employees were listening to their needs. Responding to a customer's specific, idiosyncratic needs requires comprehending those needs in the first place. So while attending to and understanding needs are key facets of listening, using concrete language takes it one step further. It *shows* listening.*

Listening is important, but if the goal is making others happy, showing we're listening is often just as key. Even if we heard what a partner or client said, for them to internalize that, we have to respond in a way that demonstrates we understood. And concrete language is one way to do that.

When our partner talks about a tough day at the office, for example, it's easy to say something like "That must have been tough" or "What a drag." But such responses are so abstract that they're less likely to have the intended impact. They're so general that they don't show we actually care.

---

* Note that the concrete language must also be relevant to the situation at hand. If a customer complains about poorly made shoes and the agent uses concrete language that is completely irrelevant (e.g., "Happy to find that jacket for you."), it wouldn't increase customer satisfaction. In fact, it would probably decrease it. It's only when the concrete language signals that the other person attended to and understood what you said that it's actually effective.

Concrete language is more effective. "I can't believe the vice president showed up forty-five minutes late" or "How frustrating that the projector didn't work." Using concrete language shows that we listened, and we care.

The same goes for interacting with clients. Using concrete language shows that we understood the specifics and can build on or respond to them.

Signaling listening is one benefit of concrete language, but it turns out there are others.

Using concrete language to present ideas, for example, makes them easier to understand.[2] Similarly, analysis of thousands of tech support pages found that pages that used more concrete language were rated as more helpful. Compared to using more abstract language (e.g., "About the security partial trust allow list") using more concrete language (e.g., "How to split and move the keyboard" or "Check your battery and charge your watch") made it easier for readers to understand what the content was about and find it more helpful in resolving their questions.

Concrete language also makes things more memorable. Readers are more likely to remember concrete phrases (e.g., "rusty engine") and sentences (e.g., "when an airplane blasts down the runway and passengers lurch backward in their seats") than abstract ones (e.g., "available knowledge" or "moving air will push up against a surface placed at an angle to the airflow").[3]

Not surprisingly, then, using concrete language has a host of beneficial consequences. It holds people's attention, encourages support, and drives desired action.[4]

In fact, linguistic concreteness even affects parole board decisions. When prisoners apologize for their actions, those who give more concrete explanations for their transgressions are more likely to be granted parole.

MAKE THE ABSTRACT CONCRETE

Given all the benefits of concrete language, one question is: Why we don't use it more often? After all, if concrete language makes things easier to understand, remember, and feel positively toward, why would anyone ever speak or write abstractly?

Whenever we express an idea, we tend to know a lot about the thing we're talking about. Salespeople know all the benefits of their product or service, teachers are experts on the material they're teaching, and managers have spent months thinking through the details of a new strategic initiative. In some ways, this knowledge is a blessing. By knowing the ins and outs of a product or service, we can zero in on the best-selling points for a particular potential client. Through being versed in a particular subject, we can bring in related ideas to help students comprehend the topic. And by spending time thinking through a new initiative, we often know exactly what's needed to help make the implementation successful.

But while knowledge can sometimes be a blessing, it can also be a curse. Because once people know a lot about something, it can be difficult for them to remember what it's like *not* to know that much. To imagine what it's like not having that depth of understanding.

When estimating what others know or don't know, people often use their own knowledge as a starting point. They assume that others know just as much as them. When talking to their colleagues about a new initiative, for example, managers usually use their own level of comprehension as an anchor. All the nuances of digital transformation are pretty easy for me to understand, so others must be having the same experience, and it's easy for them to understand as well.

As a result, we often communicate using acronyms, shorthand, and other lingo. Words, phrases, or language that other experts should be able to understand.

But what we forget is that while it's easy for us to parse, others may not feel the same way. While we have spent lots of time thinking about something, or know a lot about it, we often fail to account for the fact that others may not be in the same position.

Consequently, we often talk in ways that fly right over their heads. Think about the last time you spoke to a financial adviser, for example, or went to a mechanic. They might have talked about how a particular investment was "not a true called capital" or talked about how "the driveshaft is rated for the stock horsepower and torque, but the vehicle is currently pumping out a lot more power than stock." Things that were clearly second nature for them but left us wondering if they were speaking a second language.

This curse has a name, and appropriately, it is called the curse of knowledge.[5] It's a curse because the more we know, the more we assume others know, and thus the more we end up communicating in ways that are tough to understand.

And abstractness is the cause.

The more people learn more about something, the more they naturally start to think about it abstractly. Finding solutions to problems becomes "ideation." Determining why someone should buy from you becomes "identifying a value proposition." And Tyler, Maria, Derek, and hundreds of other new employees become "human capital." Mission statements, marketing plans, and culture documents are awash with such language.

But this isn't just a business problem. The same is true of almost any specialty. Mechanics speak mechanic lingo, teachers speak teacher lingo, and financial advisers speak financial adviser lingo. Even great doctors are often terrible communicators. They may understand the problem, but they use such abstract language to explain it that the solution is completely unintelligible (e.g., talking about lifestyle modifications rather than exercising more often).

We need to make the abstract concrete. Whether talking to colleagues or clients, students or sales reps, patients or program managers, we need to take abstract ideas and make them real by using concrete language. Helping people understand, and act on, what we're saying.

It's easier to understand what someone is saying when they talk about a phone, rather than a device. Describing a car as sporty, red, or a roadster should make it more vivid. And rather than saying we'll "go" to the back of the store to look for a larger size, using more imaginable and

Less Concrete		More Concrete
Pants	➡	Jeans
Refund	➡	Money back
Furniture	➡	Table
That	➡	T-shirt
Really	➡	Mouthwateringly
Nicely	➡	Warmly
Go	➡	Walk
Solve	➡	Fix

specific language (e.g., "walk") will help convince consumers we're going to do our best to address their issue.

Below are some more examples of more and less concrete language and check out http://textanalyzer.org/ to measure concreteness in any text.

KNOW WHEN IT'S BETTER TO BE ABSTRACT

So far, we've talked about why concrete language is beneficial. It signals listening, makes things easier to comprehend, and can even help generate more effective apologies.

But is concrete language always good? Or might there be some situations in which abstract language is better?

Everywhere you turn, there is another startup with a huge valuation. In 2007, Brian Chesky and Joe Gebbia couldn't afford the rent on their San Francisco apartment, so they rented out air mattresses on their living room floor to people coming to the city for a big design conference. Now their company, Airbnb, is worth more than $100 billion. Two friends were complaining about how tough it was to find a cab, so they turned that insight into the ride-hailing app Uber, worth close to the same amount. Dropbox, DoorDash, Stitch Fix, ClassPass, Robinhood, Warby Parker, Grammarly, Instacart, and Allbirds are only a handful of the hundreds of unicorn startups worth over a billion dollars.

But before a startup can become a unicorn, one of the first things entrepreneurs have to do is raise money. Beyond having an idea, they have to convince early-stage investors to chip in funds so that they can begin to build a business.

And raising money is tough. Famed technology startup accelerator

Y Combinator receives applications from more than twenty thousand startups a year and funds fewer than a couple hundred. Most venture capital funds support even fewer.

Founders create pitch decks, draft presentations, and submit applications for funding, but what makes some pitches more successful than others? Why do some garner support when so many others fail?

In 2020, a Harvard Business School professor and her colleagues analyzed a year's worth of funding requests.[6] A venture capital firm was looking to take an equity stake in early-stage companies interested in scaling. Fledgling businesses who were poised for long-term growth. The firm was willing to invest up to $2 million in each startup initially, with the possibility of increasing to $5 million to $10 million in subsequent funding rounds.

Not surprisingly, the firm received lots of applications—more than a thousand from companies focused on everything from technology and finance to medicine and B2B services. In addition to providing information about their company and its founding team, applicants also provided an executive summary of the business.

The pitch by a company building a wearable device to track blood alcohol content, for example, said:

> Most social drinkers can identify with the experience of waking up after a night out and wishing they had had at least one less drink . . . They may have a hangover . . . have blown their diet . . . [or] may not remember aspects of the night. But they are not addicted; they don't want to quit drinking but they wish they had the tools to find the line between enjoying drinking and waking up not feeling good. [We give] users those tools.

The pitch by a financial technology company focused on equipment leasing said:

> [Our goal] is to develop a fast solution for small and midsized companies to address the coming changes in accounting for leases expected to occur over the next four to five years . . . current lease accounting rules were developed over thirty years ago, and enabled lessees to take most of their leases off balance sheet. These rules have been criticized for many years . . . because they don't reflect the true financial position of companies. A recent exposure draft from the Accounting Standards Bodies addresses this by requiring lessees to capitalize their leases. In other words—bring them on the balance sheet.

Investors read through the pitches and sorted out what to do. They decided whether each startup had growth potential (was highly scalable) and determined whether or not to consider the firm for potential funding.

To understand what drove funding decisions, the researchers examined a variety of factors. They measured what industry each startup was in, whether it targeted businesses or consumers, whether it offered a product or service, and the size of the founding team.

Not surprisingly, aspects of the business itself played an important role. Some industries were seen as having high growth potential, while others not as much. Similarly, what the startups were offering mattered as well. Compared to services, products were seen as easier to scale.

Beyond the company itself, though, and the business area it focused on, the researchers also analyzed the pitches—what applicants said and how they said it.

One might expect that pitch language shouldn't matter much. After all, the success of an investment depends a lot more on what business the company is in, or whether they have a strong leadership team.

But even controlling for those factors, pitch language had a strong impact on investment decisions. Pitches that used more abstract language made investors think the company had more potential for growth and greater ability to scale. Abstract language also boosted the likelihood of investment, increasing the chance startups made it through the initial round of consideration for funding.*

In some ways, this is pretty surprising. After all, venture capitalists are seasoned veterans who've invested tens of millions of dollars in dozens of startups. They've seen businesses go public for billions and they've seen ideas fall apart in a matter of months. So the fact that something as simple as the language founders used shaped decision making is striking.

But even more surprising is the *type* of language that increased investment. After all, concrete language increases understanding, boosts memorability, and has a host of other benefits. So given all that, why did *less* concrete (more abstract) language increase funding?

The answer, it turns out, has to do with what concrete language communicates about potential. As we've discussed, concrete language often relates to observable aspects of items, actions, and events. Things that exist in the here and now that we can see, touch, or feel.

---

* This is also one reason that female founders tend to have a harder time raising venture capital. Women tend to use more concrete language and pitch the business they're building right now, whereas men tend to use more abstract language, describing a broader vision of how they see their business expanding over time. As one venture capitalist put it, "I see men pitch unicorns and women pitch businesses."

Consequently, concrete language is often quite helpful. It can help people visualize what is being said and understand complex topics. In the context of pitch language, for example, using concrete language should help potential investors understand what a company does and the immediate problems that it hopes to solve.

But when deciding whether to fund a startup, understanding isn't the main thing investors are looking for. They're not just trying to comprehend a business, they're trying to forecast its potential—not just whether it will survive but whether or not it will flourish. How likely is this business to grow in the future? Not just a little, but a lot? How easy will it be to scale up?

And while concrete language is great for increasing understanding, or for making complex topics easier to comprehend, when it comes to things like such as describing a company's growth potential, abstract language is better, because while concrete language focuses on the tangible here and now, abstract language gets into the bigger picture.

Take Uber, the company best known for its ride-hailing app. When Uber was founded in 2009, it would have been easy to describe the business as exactly that: "A smartphone app that makes it easier to get a taxi, connecting passengers and drivers and reducing wait time." This description is perfectly accurate and provides a good sense of what the company does. It's also highly concrete. It uses specific language to help people understand the nature of Uber's business.

But that's not the only way Uber could be described. In fact, one of the cofounders actually positioned the company quite differently. He described it as "a transportation solution that is convenient, reliable, and readily accessible to everyone."

In some ways, the difference might seem minor. Both descriptions give some sense of the general space Uber is in and what it's trying to do.

But while the first description is quite concrete, the way the cofounder actually pitched the business is much more abstract. Rather than focusing on ride hailing per se, which is much narrower in scope, calling Uber a "transportation solution" taps the broader problem Uber is trying to solve.

That, in turn, increased investment because it made the potential market seem much larger. A ride-hailing app? I can think of a few people who might need that or a few situations in which it might be useful.

But a transportation solution? Wow, that seems a lot broader. Lots of people and companies could use something like that, and it seems to have lots of applications.*

We're not just a fintech startup, we're a solutions provider. We're not just a device builder, we're a life improver.

Rather than focusing on one niche, abstract language makes the market seem widespread. And given that larger growth potential, a company seems like a much more promising investment.

Consequently, whether it's better to use concrete or abstract language depends on the outcome we're trying to achieve.

Want to help people understand a complex idea, feel heard, or remember what was said? Using concrete language is going to be more effective. Using verbs that focus on actions (e.g., walk, talk, help, or improve), for example, rather than adjectives (e.g., honest, aggressive, or helpful). Talking about physical objects or using evocative language to help them see what we're saying.

---

* Using abstract language also makes founders seem like forward-looking visionaries, focused not just on the venture as it exists at the moment but how it might exist in the future; not just what it is but what it could be. They have a broad vision of what might be possible and how their business might grow or expand over time.

But if we want people to think our idea has potential, or that we're a forward-thinking visionary, abstract language is more effective.

Abstract language also suggests that communicators are more powerful and would be better managers or leaders.[7] Using abstract language to describe everyday activities (e.g., describing ignoring someone as "showing dislike" rather than "not saying hello") makes people seem more focused on the big picture, and thus more powerful, dominant, and in control. Similarly, hearing someone describe a product more abstractly (i.e., "nutritious" rather than "containing lots of vitamins") made them seem more fit to be a manager or leader.

Would abstract language be as memorable or help listeners understand a complex idea? Probably not. But if they were deciding who to vote for, or promote to a managerial role, abstract language would be more likely to move them in the right direction.

More generally, when trying to make language either more concrete or more abstract, one helpful approach is to focus on either the *how* or the *why*.

Want to be more concrete? Focus on the *how*. How does a product meet consumer needs? How does a proposed new initiative address an important problem? Thinking about *how* something is or will be done encourages concreteness. It focuses on the feasibility and helps generate concrete descriptions.

Want to be more abstract? Focus on the *why*. Why does a product meet consumer needs? Why does a proposed new initiative address an important problem? Thinking about *why* something is good or right encourages abstractness. It focuses on its desirability and helps generate abstract descriptions.

Making Magic

It's easy to talk abstractly. Particularly when we know a lot about something, we tend to communicate in a high-level way that we think is easy to understand.

Unfortunately, however, this often misses the mark. Consequently, we need to harness the power of linguistic concreteness.

1. **Make people feel heard.** Want to show someone you're listening? Be concrete. Give specific details that show we paid attention and understood.
2. **Be concrete.** Don't just pick things that sound good, use words that listeners can see in their minds. It's a lot easier to imagine a red sportscar than ideation.
3. **Know when it's better to be abstract.** Thinking about the nuts and bolts of how something will happen, and focusing on specific actions, makes things concrete.

But while concrete language is often useful, if our goal is to come off as powerful, or make something seem like it has growth potential, using abstract language is better. In those cases:

1. **Focus on the why.** Thinking about the reasoning behind something helps things stay high level and communicate that big picture.

In sum, whether we want to help people understand what we're saying, make them feel heard, or deepen engagement, the language of concreteness can help.

So far, we've talked about how words can activate identity and agency, convey confidence, enable us to ask the right questions, and leverage concreteness. Next, we examine a fifth type of magic word: words that express emotion.

5

Employ Emotion

Growing up in West Covina, California, Guy Raz dreamed of becoming a journalist. There was nothing he wanted more than to be a print reporter, and the best and brightest started at places like the *Chicago Tribune*, so that was where he applied.

But it turned him down. As did the *Dallas Morning News*, the *Baltimore Sun*, and other newspapers he applied to. No one would hire him.

So at age twenty-two, while many of his fellow graduates were taking high-paying jobs in consulting or finance, Guy took a position on the other end of the pay scale. As an intern. And since he couldn't get a job in the print world, he ended up accepting an internship on a radio program.

Guy still hoped to be a reporter, though, so in his spare time, he wrote freelance articles for whoever would take them. He placed an article here and there, mostly in a free alternative weekly paper in Washington, DC.

He kept at it, worked hard, and moved up. He became a production assistant, a studio director, and eventually a foreign correspondent. He covered Eastern Europe and the Balkans, became CNN's Jerusalem correspondent, and then returned to the United States to cover the Pentagon and the US military.

Flash forward to today, and even if you don't recognize Guy's name, you've probably heard his voice. In 2013, Guy became the host and editorial director of the *TED Radio Hour*. In 2016, he started the entrepreneurship podcast *How I Built This*, and since then he has founded and hosted other popular programs like *Wisdom from the Top*, *Wow in the World*, and *The Rewind*. He is the first person in the history of podcasting to have three of the twenty most downloaded shows, reaches more than 20 million listeners a month, and has been described as one of the most popular podcasters in history.

Listen to one of Guy's podcasts, and it's clear why they're so popular. Guy is an amazing storyteller. Hearing him talk, it's hard not to pay attention.

But while some topics are just naturally compelling, Guy has an uncanny ability to turn *anything* into a riveting narrative. From the invention of a vacuum cleaner to the founding of a soap company. From German astronomers to how our sense of smell works.

Through his years as a foreign correspondent, Guy honed his craft. Finding the personal stories and human dramas that were behind the biggest news of the day.

Along the way, he realized that great stories often have things in common. Ingredients or guidelines that help make anything more engaging. And to begin to explore what those things are, it helps to start with one of Guy's interviews that was starting to go sideways.

———————————

A few years ago, Guy was interviewing Dave Anderson, a promi-
nent Native American entrepreneur. Among other ventures, Dave had
founded Famous Dave's, the legendary pit barbecue chain, and helped
form Rainforest Café, a family-themed restaurant group.

As with all episodes of *How I Built This*, the interview set out to
cover the story of Dave's success. How Dave went from having one barbecue shack in a town of 2,300 people to building a culinary empire
with nearly two hundred locations.

But Guy kept digging into the failures. How Dave failed as an oil
salesman. How his flower business had gone under. How the board of
directors of Famous Dave's had refused to give Dave a seat at the table
after he had left the company and wanted to return.

Dave started getting tense. Soon he became visibly frustrated. Then,
in the middle of the interview, he stopped and exclaimed, "Why do
you keep asking me about all my failures!?"

Dave had been caught off guard. He had been expecting the interview
to be a highlight reel and felt like Guy was trying to make him look
bad. He wasn't keen on sharing a compendium of his greatest mistakes,
particularly in front of millions of listeners. Needless to say, he hated the
interview and left quite upset.

Dave's not alone. Particularly in public settings, we want to focus
attention on our successes. Accounts won, sales increased, and people
persuaded. The highlights or high notes. Social media is a veritable
greatest hits album. This person got promoted, that person is in Barba-
dos, someone else got a new car/award/important recognition.

We think that promoting such a curated, varnished perspective will
make people like us. They'll think that we're more impressive, worth
getting to know, or worth hiring.

Is that intuition actually correct?

WHEN IMPERFECTIONS ARE AN ASSET

In 1966, some behavioral scientists conducted an experiment on making mistakes.[1] They asked University of Minnesota students to listen to tape recordings of a "contestant" (actually an actor) trying out for the college trivia team.

Unfortunately, the contestant wasn't very qualified. He answered only 30 percent of quiz questions correctly and didn't seem that sharp.

Further, to make matters worse, for some of the students the contestant made yet another mistake: he clumsily spilled coffee all over his brand-new suit.

Some students listened to a tape where the contestant spilled coffee on himself, others listened to a tape where he didn't.

Not surprisingly, making a mistake hurt students' impression of the contestant. Listeners had less positive impressions of him when he spilled coffee on himself than when he didn't.

But mistakes weren't *always* bad. Because when different students were given information about a contestant that was highly qualified in the first place (i.e., he answered 92 percent of quiz questions correctly), in those cases, a mistake made them like the contestant *more*, not less.

Same coffee, same spilling it all over himself, different impact.

The study revealed that mistakes themselves are neither good nor bad. Their impact hinges on the broader context. When incompetent people made mistakes, it just reinforced other's already negative impressions. It was more of the same.

When competent people made mistakes, though, it had the opposite effect. Successful people are hard to identify with. They seem so perfect that it's hard to connect. And that's why mistakes can help. Because when otherwise competent people make a mistake once in a while, it humanizes them. It makes them more real, which makes them more likable.

This so called "pratfall effect" is why Guy wanted to ask Dave about some of the rough spots. Guy wasn't trying to embarrass him. Or air his dirty laundry. Guy just wanted to humanize Dave. To make him more relatable.

Because if all people know about someone is that they did successful thing after successful thing, it's hard to empathize. They seem so different that it's hard to relate. But if they failed here, or overcame adversity there, suddenly it's easier to connect.

Indeed, in the weeks that followed the airing of the episode, dozens of friends, colleagues, and customers reached out to Dave to thank him for his honesty. Most of them had known about his success, but they hadn't realized the challenges he had gone through to get where he was. And hearing about those difficulties, those tough times, gave them inspiration and hope. That anything was possible.

The pratfall effect shows that imperfections can be an asset. But it's actually just one example of a much larger phenomenon. And that is the value of employing emotion.

Four ways to do that are to: (1) build a roller coaster, (2) mix up moments, (3) consider the context, and (4) activate uncertainty.

BUILD A ROLLER COASTER

Stories are an integral part of everyday life. We tell stories about how a meeting went, what we did this weekend, or why we think we're perfect for a particular job. We tell stories to make a point, sell an idea, or just connect with friends. And when we're not telling stories, we're consuming them, through books, movies, shows, and podcasts.

Some stories, though, are better than others. They're more interesting, engaging, and captivating. Rather than lulling the audience to sleep, or leading them to look for something else to do, listeners are on the edge of their proverbial seats, waiting to find out what happens next.

Not surprisingly, then, people have long speculated about what makes a good story. Kurt Vonnegut, for example, author of *Slaughterhouse-Five* and *Cat's Cradle*, suggested that "stories have shapes which can be drawn on graph paper."* In his master's thesis, "rejected because it was so simple and looked like too much fun," Vonnegut theorized that the ups and downs that characters go through could be graphed to reveal that story's shape.

Take the classic tale of Cinderella. The kindhearted heroine sees her world turned upside down when her beloved mother dies. Cinderella's father remarries, and his new wife has two wicked stepdaughters who mistreat Cinderella constantly. As if that weren't enough, he soon dies, leaving her to serve as her wicked stepmother's maid.

But just when all looks lost, things get better. Cinderella meets her fairy godmother, goes to a ball, and falls in love with a handsome prince. Unfortunately, she's forced to run away from the ball at the stroke of midnight, and her stepmother tries to stop the prince from finding her,

---

* Though Vonnegut may have been one of the first to articulate this idea so persuasively, the topic itself is an ancient one. In the fourth century BC, Aristotle argued that all stories had common patterns, or trajectories, and could be divided into three key parts. In 1863, Gustav Freytag, a German writer, built on Aristotle's model and suggested that dramas could be divided into five parts: an introduction, rising action, a climax, falling action, and a denouement. More recently, everyone from narrative theorists and linguists to literary scholars and so-called script doctors has theorized about plot structure and story shapes.

but in the end, Cinderella and the prince are reunited, and the story ends happily ever after.

Vonnegut might have drawn the shape of Cinderella's story to be something like this:

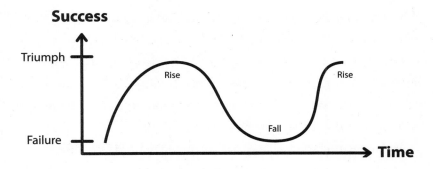

The story starts negatively. Cinderella's parents have died, and she is a maid for her cruel stepmother. Things start to improve (she gets invited to a ball and meets a prince), but then they get worse (she has to run off at the stroke of midnight). Eventually the story ends on a high note.

Given the importance of stories, the idea that stories have shapes is a fascinating one. And in the decades that followed Vonnegut's suggestion, the concept captured popular imagination. Videos of Vonnegut talking about different shapes went viral, and major news outlets breathlessly claimed that all stories in the world could be captured by a few common patterns.

But while the notion of story shapes is intriguing, actually identifying such shapes is a bit more challenging. Some have suggested that the story of Cinderella looks one way, for example, while others have suggested completely different shapes.

Further, even if stories do have shapes, that begs the question of whether those shapes actually matter. It's one thing to note that there are different types of stories, but it's another to see whether certain ways of telling stories actually make them more engaging and impactful.

To answer these questions, some colleagues and I dived into the science of stories. We started by analyzing tens of thousands of movies, everything from blockbusters such as *Forrest Gump* and *The Matrix* to small indie films such as *The Marsh* and *An Invisible Sign*. We looked at newer movies such as *The Hunger Games* and *Argo* and older movies such as *Jaws* and the original *Star Wars*.

And to quantify their shapes, we analyzed the words they used.[2]

Some words are more positive than others. Words such as "laughter," "happiness," "love," and "rainbow" are pretty positive.[3] They often appear in positive situations, and most people feel positively when they hear them.

Words like "pandemic," "funeral," "cruel," and "cry," on the other hand, are more negative. They represent undesirable things that make most people feel negatively.

Words like "anyway," "repeat," and "Pittsburgh" are somewhere in between. They are used in both positive and negative situations and don't make most people feel particularly happy or sad (unless you happen to love or hate Pittsburgh).

We broke each movie script into dozens of pieces, each a few hundred words long, and averaged the positivity of the words in each part.*

---

* Though one might wonder whether such measures are accurate, they're highly correlated with human judgments. So chunks of text that were rated as more positive or negative tended to be seen the same way by people.

Parts that talked about a character finding their lost love, reuniting with friends, or discovering a lost treasure were scored as relatively positive, while parts that talked about a rough breakup, an argument, or the hero almost dying would be scored more negatively.

Then, we used these scores to plot each movie's emotional trajectory. Similar to the figure of the story of Cinderella, how positive or negative things were at different parts of the narrative.

To get a sense of what this looks like, here is the emotional trajectory of the original *Star Wars*.

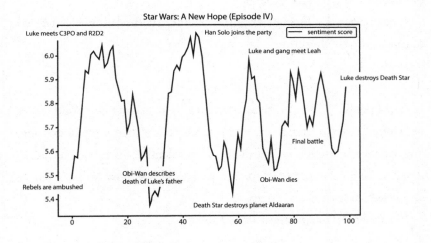

The main character, Luke Skywalker, is sent on a quest to save Princess Leia and defeat the evil Galactic Empire. There are positive parts, like when Luke befriends Han Solo and when he rescues Princess Leia and escapes from the Death Star. But there are also negative parts, including when Luke's parents are killed and when Luke's mentor sacrifices himself to allow others to escape. In the end, though, the story ends on a positive note: Luke, aided by his mentor's voice, destroys the enemy ship and celebrates victory with his friends.*

One positive or negative word doesn't reveal much, but examining hundreds of words together gives a decent sense of what is happening. When Luke's friend is killed or their uncle's farm is destroyed, lots of other negative words are being used. Characters are sad or crying, or filled with hate or fear. When the villain is killed though, or his ship is destroyed, the surrounding words are more upbeat. Characters are celebrating, cheering, dancing or hugging, and the language is a lot more positive. The words in the script reveal the nature of the action, without our even having to watch the movie.

Once mapped, we could examine whether successful movies tended to follow certain patterns.

Most people prefer positive experiences to negative ones. We'd rather be promoted than fired, eat a tasty lunch rather than a mediocre one, and visit with friends rather than see the dentist. In fact, if asked to describe an ideal day, most people would fill it with positive experiences and leave out the negative ones.

But that's not what makes a good story.

Imagine a narrative where everything was just plain wonderful. The main character was beloved by all, anything they wanted came easily, and they frolicked through fields of sunflowers while birds sang them

---

* This measure isn't perfect. The word "kill," for example, shows up both when the hero *kills* the villain (a really positive moment) and when someone *kills* the hero's best friend (a really negative moment). Similarly, the word "destroy" doesn't distinguish between whether the thing destroyed was the villain's ship or the hero's uncle's farm. But though it may be difficult to determine exactly what is true of individual words, in aggregate, the sentiment expressed by groups of words provides a good sense of whether a positive or negative thing is happening.

songs of happiness. The emotional trajectory might look something like this:

Positive

Negative

That might make a great life insurance commercial, but a movie? Potential viewers would probably go search for something more interesting to watch.

Because while people generally prefer positive personal experiences to negative ones, when reading books or watching movies, endless positivity would be pretty boring. When it comes to stories, tension is key. Will Cinderella and the prince end up happily ever after, or will she be stuck washing floors for the rest of her life? Will Luke and the Rebel Alliance destroy the Death Star, or will the dark side prevail? If the answers were obvious, we wouldn't need to finish the story. But because it's not clear what will happen, we stay tuned to find out.

Along these lines, many successful stories seem to follow a similar structure. Characters have to overcome various trials and tribulations before they reach a happy ending. In both Star Wars and Harry Potter, for example, the hero must overcome the death of his parents. He makes friends along the way and things start looking up, but then something bad happens, and so on. Each barrier or bump along the road is something the character must deal with before they reach their final destination.

In these and similar examples, the emotional trajectory seems to follow a wavelike pattern. Like a mountain range, long climbs up to high points followed by long descents down to low points. Then back up again.

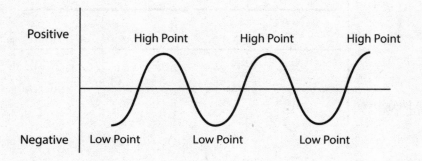

Indeed, when we analyzed the movies, we found that those which interspersed highly positive moments with strongly negative ones were more successful. Movies that repeatedly traversed from the lowest of emotional lows to the highest of emotional highs, and back again, were liked more.

The most engaging episodes of *How I Built This* follow a similar pattern. An entrepreneur has a promising idea, something they think will change the world, but then a key supplier backs out at the last minute. The entrepreneur pushes through the challenge, and starts to get some sales, but just when they're finally gaining traction, a big retailer cancels its order. Like opposing weights on a scale, positive things are soon balanced out by negative ones.

This pattern is one reason Guy is such a great storyteller. Sure, he asks entrepreneurs about their successes. The clients they convinced, stores they built, and customers they attracted.

But he also asks them about their failures. The stuff that didn't work.

The money they lost. The dead ends they pursued. The rejections they suffered.

Because interspersing these low points among the high ones does more than just humanize successful people. It builds a better story.

Hearing about someone who started a company, grew it fast, and sold it for $100 million just isn't that exciting. Not only is it not that surprising, few people can relate. Most of us have never had such immediate and continued success.

But hearing about an entrepreneur who went through seven years of building prototype after prototype, only to be turned down at every step of the way? Or learning about someone who was turned down by 279 retailers before the 280th finally said yes?

Now, that's more interesting.

Low points, or depths of despair, make the high points that much more powerful. It's nice to see Cinderella and the prince live happily ever after, just like it's nice to see someone's business take off. But that happiness is even sweeter when it feels like the story could just have easily ended differently.* Victories are savored more when they're snatched from the jaws of defeat.

THE VALUE OF VOLATILITY

Highlighting the hurdles, or going from low to high, and back again, makes stories more engaging. But we also found something else. Consider these story trajectories.

---

* Not only is the story more engaging, but it makes listeners feel that they can overcome adversity in their own lives. After all, if that person did it, why can't I?

Story 1

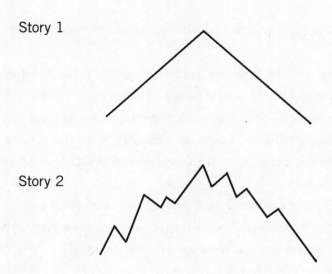

Story 2

The highs and lows are the same, but the emotional trajectories are quite distinct. In Story 1, the ride is smooth. Moments are increasingly positive until the apex when things turn around. The ride might be steep, but it's consistent.

Story 2, however, is a lot bumpier. The peak is the same, but rather than continuously increasing and then decreasing, the trajectory is more jagged. Things move in a positive direction but then get more negative before turning positive again.

Which is better, a smooth ride or bumpy one?

Humans are amazingly adept at acclimating to whatever situation they find themselves in. Getting dumped or fired is bad when it happens, but we quickly bounce back, finding the silver lining and looking toward more positive futures.

The same holds for positive things. Getting our dream job or house is great at first, but the initial excitement soon subsides.

Take winning the lottery. Imagine winning not just five or ten dollars but something more substantial: hundreds of thousands of dollars or, even better, a few million. How would that feel? Do you think it would make you happier?

When asked how experiences like winning the lottery would impact their happiness, most people give the same answer: "Are you crazy? Or *course* it would make me happier. Winning millions of dollars would be fantastic. I could pay my bills, buy that sports car, maybe even quit my job. Winning the lottery would make me a *lot* happier."

But while the benefits of winning benefits seem obvious, the reality is a bit more complex. In fact, numerous studies find that winning the lottery, even when the sums are substantial, has little to no impact on happiness.[4]

At some level this seems crazy. How could winning a huge amount of money *not* boost happiness? Hundreds of millions of people buy lottery tickets, all with the hope of winning. How could realizing their dream not make people happier?

Decades of research on so-called hedonic adaptation, however, has found that people adapt to their situation.[5] Whether looking at positive things, like winning the lottery, or negative ones, like being injured in a major accident, people adjust and eventually return to their normal level of happiness.

And because people tend to adapt, interrupting positive things with negative ones can actually increase enjoyment. Take commercials. Most people hate them, so removing them should make shows or other entertainment more enjoyable.

But the opposite is true. Shows are actually *more* enjoyable when they're broken up by annoying commercials.[6] Because these less enjoyable moments break up adaptation to the positive experience of the show.

Think about eating chocolate chips. The first chip is delicious: sweet, melt-in-your-mouth goodness. The second chip is also pretty good. But by the fourth, fifth, or tenth chip in a row, the goodness is no longer as pleasurable. We adapt.

Interspersing positive experiences with less positive ones, however, can slow adaptation. Eating a Brussels sprout between chocolate chips or viewing commercials between parts of TV shows disrupts the process. The less positive moment makes the following positive one new again and thus more enjoyable.

Something similar happens in stories. In finance, "volatility" describes the variability of a stock, asset, or market. More volatile assets have greater swings in valuation. Sometimes they go up, sometimes they go down, but they're so erratic that it's hard to know what will happen when.

The same goes for narratives. Emotionally volatile stories are unpredictable. Things might generally be getting better, but at any moment it's hard to know whether they'll get better or worse. Returning to the two stories shown previously, Story 2 is much more volatile.

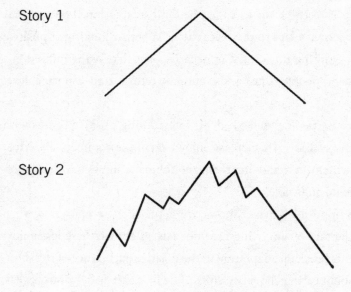

And this unpredictability makes the ride more stimulating and increases liking. Indeed, when we analyzed thousands of movies, we found that volatility made stories better. Audiences are dialed in to find out what will happen next, and, as a result, enjoy the experience more.

Great stories, then, are a bit like roller coasters. First, as we discussed earlier, a flat ride isn't that interesting. Big highs and lows make things more fun.

Beyond such peaks, though, moment-to-moment changes also matter. Is this the moment when the bottom drops out? Are we halfway up to the top or almost there? That uncertainty makes the ride all the more engaging.*

Taken together, these findings about emotional language have some clear implications. First, imperfections can be an asset. Whether in job interviews, or other public settings, people often feel the need to come off as perfect, to sweep mistakes under the rug.

But that's not always the best course of action. As long as someone is already perceived as competent, acknowledging mistakes can be beneficial. Among job candidates who are already doing well (coming in for their second interview), for example, openly admitting past mistakes made them more likable, not less. Not only does taking ownership demonstrate responsibility, it makes people seem more relatable.

---

* Writers and producers say you can't boil down something as complex as a movie into just a couple of data points. And they're right. Movies are complex, and their success depends on a host of things; acting, cinematography, music, directing, and plot are just a handful of them. The story can be great, but if the casting is wrong or the directing is off, the story won't sing. But just saying movies are complex misses the point. Just because they're complicated doesn't mean that there aren't certain approaches that tend to make them better.

Revealing a past shortcoming can similarly help a competent manager become better liked among their team.

The slip-up, though, should be relatively minor. Spilling something on one's jacket or making a small mistake can make people more relatable. A mistake that is more central to the job at hand will likely be viewed more negatively.

Second, leverage failure. When asked to tell their story, explain their background, or otherwise talk about themselves, people tend to focus on the highlights. They see failure as a mark of shame and think the best way to come off positively is to focus on the positives.

That intuition, though, isn't always correct. Everybody faces adversity. Everybody fails or falls short sometimes. And acknowledging those challenges makes us more relatable and helps others resonate with our story.

Third, and building on these ideas, by understanding what makes a good story, we can all become better storytellers. Most people are not born raconteurs. We're not the guy in the Irish pub who can just stand at the bar and hold an audience captive.

But with the right training and practice, great storytelling is a skill anyone can develop. By understanding how stories work, and the science behind them, we can make any story more impactful. Highlighting the hurdles—moving from lows to highs and back again—and mixing up moments—leveraging emotional volatility—can help turn any story into a great one.

CONSIDER THE CONTEXT

So far, we've talked about emotions as positive and negative. Some things feel good, and others feel bad. Words like "laughter" and "happiness" are positive while words like "hate" and "cry" are negative.

But there's another important difference that often goes unnoticed.

It's Friday night, and you're trying to pick a restaurant. You're out of town on a trip, so you're looking online to figure out where to go. One place looked promising, but it's closed for renovations. Another has interesting food but seems too far from your hotel.

Finally you come across two options that look good. Both are within walking distance, are reasonably priced, and have food you're interested in. So to make the final call, you read some online reviews.

Both restaurants have uniformly positive reviews and are rated 4.7 out of 5 stars. "This is an amazing place," a review for the first one says, "and it was enjoyable to eat there." Similarly, a review for the second restaurant says, "This is a perfect place, and it was worthwhile to eat there."

Which restaurant would you pick?

If you said the first one, you're not alone. When hundreds of people were asked to make a similar choice, 65 percent chose the first option. And the reason has to do with the difference between positivity and emotionality.

When choosing a restaurant, buying a product, or making choices more generally, we often consider others' reactions. Did they like the restaurant or hate it? Are the reviews positive or negative?

This makes sense. We want to eat at good restaurants and avoid bad ones. We want to buy things people like and avoid things people hate. Consequently, the more positive others' opinions are, the more we think we'll feel similarly.

But seeing things as positive or negative, or good or bad, only goes so far. Nearly half of all restaurant reviews on Yelp are 5 stars, for example, and the average product rating on Amazon is 4.2 out of 5 stars. Most products and services get a 4- or 5-star review, making it hard to learn much from the ratings.

Further, higher star ratings aren't always diagnostic. Looking at more than a hundred product categories, for example, researchers found only a small relationship between product quality and Amazon ratings.[7] Similarly, in many book genres, higher ratings have little relationship to sales.[8]

So if positivity alone isn't always diagnostic of quality or success, what is?

Below are some pairs of words that express the same general sentiment, or positivity.

Beautiful and Best

Mindblowing and Noteworthy

Childish and Unclear

Repulsive and Dumb

"Beautiful" and "best," for example, suggest that something is really good, and "mindblowing" and "noteworthy" suggest that something is good, but not as good as "beautiful" and "best." In fact, when hundreds of people were asked to rate various words on their positivity, "beautiful" and "best" both scored 8.4 out of 9, thus ranking among the most positive words listed.

The same is true of the more negative pairs. "Repulsive" and "dumb" both suggest something is really bad, and "childish" and "unclear" both suggest that something is bad, but not as bad as "repulsive" and "dumb."

But while the words in each pair express the same level of goodness or badness, they vary on another dimension. Their *emotionality*, or the degree to which they express an attitude based on feelings or emotional reactions.[9]

Whenever people express an attitude or opinion, they can do so in various ways. They can say they *loved, hated, liked,* or *avoided* a movie, or they can say that a restaurant was *awesome, amazing, mediocre,* or *terrible.* Food can be *delicious* or *disgusting,* service can be *stellar* or *subpar,* and can be *electrifying* or *excellent.*

These words not only indicate how much someone liked something, they also suggest what that evaluation is based on (i.e., emotions versus other factors).

Take a restaurant. If someone says they *enjoy* the food, or they *love* the ambiance, it suggests their opinion is based on their feelings. Their emotional reaction to the place. If they say the food is *healthy,* or *reasonably priced,* however, they still like it, but it suggests that their opinion is based more on their thoughts.

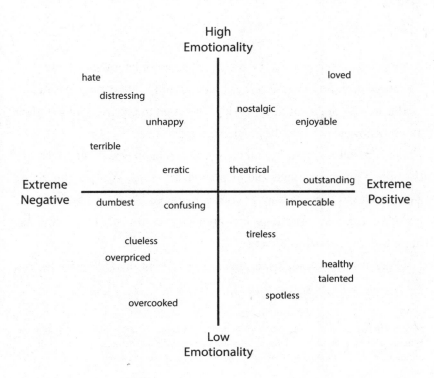

The same goes for a car. If someone says it's *fun* to drive, or looks *amazing*, their opinion is based more on feelings. If they say it's *well built* or gets good *gas mileage*, feelings are playing less of a role.

Overall then, words can be arrayed based not only on their positivity and negativity, or goodness and badness, but also on their emotionality, or whether or not they suggest a feelings-based response.

Restaurants with more emotional reviews get more reservations, movies with more emotional reviews do better at the box office, and books with more emotional reviews sell more copies.[10] Using emotional language suggests people have stronger attitudes, which may lead their experiences to have a bigger effect on others.[11]

But rather than always being persuasive, whether emotional language encourages action depends on is the *type of thing* we're trying to persuade people about.

Products or services can be described as more hedonic or more utilitarian. Music, flowers, and other hedonic things are consumed for the pleasure and enjoyment they provide. We listen to music because it's fun and buy flowers because they make us happy.

Glue, gasoline, toasters, and other utilitarian objects, in contrast, are consumed for more functional or practical reasons. We buy glue to fix a chair, get gas because it makes our car run, and buy a toaster to, well, make toast. Utilitarian things are often more cognitive or instrumental in nature, purchased to fill a need.*

When researchers looked at the impact of emotional language in tens

---

* Even with the same product, certain attributes can be more utilitarian while others are more hedonic. The cushioning of running shoes, for example, or the fuel usage of a car are utilitarian attributes, while the color of the shoes or design of the car are more hedonic in nature.

of thousands of Amazon reviews, they found that emotional language had different effects in these two types of domains.[12]

As mentioned, for hedonic things (music, movies, and novels), emotional language increased impact. Emotional reviews were more helpful and made consumers more interested in making a purchase.

Returning to the restaurant choice, for example, in many ways the two restaurants were described similarly. Both use extremely positive words.

Restaurant 1	Restaurant 2
"This is an amazing place, and it was enjoyable to eat there."	"This is a perfect place, and it was worthwhile to eat there."

But while the words were similarly positive, the description of Restaurant 1 used more emotional language. The word "amazing" is more emotional than the word "perfect" and the word "enjoyable" is more emotional than the word "worthwhile."

The increased emotionality, in turn, led more people to pick that restaurant.

For utilitarian products, however, the opposite occurred. For razors, emotionality backfired. Emotional reviews were *less* helpful, made people *less* willing to purchase whatever was reviewed.

Because while emotionality is good for hedonic things, it's bad for more utilitarian ones. When picking and using hedonic products and services, emotion is a deciding factor. People want sports cars to be exciting, movies to be enjoyable, and vacations to be fun. So when emotional words are used to describe hedonic things, people think they'll like those things more.

But when picking and using utilitarian products and services, evoking emotion isn't really the goal. People want glue that hardens quickly, gas that is inexpensive, and a toaster that easily makes toast. Utilitarian things are often bought to do a job, and people pick them because their thoughts (rather than emotions) suggest they will do that job well.

Consequently, while someone might say a blender is "amazing" or "delightful," that doesn't necessarily make others want to buy it. In fact, such emotional language often backfires because it violates people's expectations around what they are looking for. So much so that it may even lower trust in what was said and the person who said it.

Overall then, it's important to not only consider language's positivity, but also its emotionality.

When marketing a product, selling an idea, or even pitching ourselves, we often use positive language. Our product is "great," our idea is "innovative," and we are "hardworking." Food is "fantastic," blockchain is "transformative," and our writing skills are "excellent." (Really. They are. I promise.)

But it's not enough to just say positive things. We need to consider the context. "Brilliant," "awesome," "excellent," and "superb" are all words that suggest something is really, really good. But they differ in the amount of emotionality they involve, and consequently, may be more or less effective depending on the context.

When marketing a product, service, or experience, for example, is it more hedonic or more utilitarian? Are people buying it for pleasure or enjoyment, or more functional or practical reasons?

If it's more about enjoyment, emotional words like "awesome" and "beautiful" fit really well. Saying a movie is "heartwarming," a destination is "inspiring," or a meditation app is "fantastic" not only suggests those things are good but does so in a way that encourages purchase and action.

If the product, service, or experience is more about practical function-
ality, however, those same positive words may backfire. Less emotional
words like "brilliant," "flawless," and "perfect" will be more persuasive.
Calling a dictation app "brilliant" rather than "awesome," for example,
should encourage purchase and use.

The same holds for describing ourselves. Whether drafting a résumé,
filling out a job application, or writing a dating profile, we are constantly
pitching ourselves to others. Sure, we should say positive things rather
than negative ones, and use words like "fun" on dating profiles but not
job applications, but it's more than that.

For things like résumés and job applications, most evaluators have a
utilitarian outlook. Like buying a product to fill a need, they're looking
for people who can solve a problem or add value.

So don't just list positive adjectives, pick the right ones. In most situations, less emotionality should be better, and emotional language may
backfire—unless the company prides itself on its company culture or
employees' being "part of the family."

Things like dating profiles, however, are usually more hedonic in nature. People aren't looking to solve a problem, they're looking for someone who will make them happy. So emotionality should be more useful.

Not just positive words, but the right *type* of positive ones.

The benefits of emotional language also vary over the course of social
interactions. Many conversations are oriented around achieving something. Meetings are about making decisions, customer service calls are
about solving a problem, and sales pitches are about closing a deal.

But although people often think it makes sense to jump into addressing the issue at hand, that's not actually the best course of action. When
we analyzed hundreds of problem-solving conversations, we found that

connecting first was key,[13] starting with warmer, more emotional language before diving into addressing the issues.

Relationship building (or maintenance) helps set the stage for whatever comes next. It strengthens social connection and builds rapport.

Consequently, warm, emotional language is particularly useful at the
beginning of a conversation. In a customer service context, for example,
phrasing a question as "How can I *help* you?" (which uses more emotional
language) rather than "How can I *solve* your issue?" is more effective.

But while starting with emotional language is beneficial, it only goes
so far. Being nice is good, but eventually decisions need to be made and
problems need to be solved.

And that is where less emotional, more cognitive language becomes
important. Indeed, when customer service agents used more emotional
language at the beginning of conversations, and more cognitive language in the middle, customers were more satisfied with the interaction
and purchased more afterward.

Don't just solve. And don't just connect.
Connect, then solve.

ACTIVATE UNCERTAINTY

Positivity and emotionality are two ways words can convey emotion
and impact attitudes and actions. But one more aspect is worth noting.

As anyone who has ever made a presentation can attest, keeping the
audience engaged is challenging. Virtual meetings have only made this
worse. The presentation is just another window on people's screen,
email is already open, and it's easy to pretend to pay attention while
doing something else.

Content creators face a similar struggle. From publishers and media companies to marketers and influencers, everyone is trying to attract and hold attention. But the sheer multitude of available options makes this increasingly difficult to achieve. News articles appear next to dozens of substitutes, and rather than reading a whole article, most people skim a little and then switch to reading something else.

Against this backdrop of endless distraction, the notion is often that "interesting" things succeed and everything else is doomed to fail. Articles about hot new tech gadgets, for example, celebrity gossip, or sports scores garner lots of attention, while weightier topics like climate change, or presentations about information security, lull everyone to sleep.

So are presenters of less engaging topics just doomed to fail? Or might there be ways to increase engagement, even for topics that seem less naturally appealing?

One common approach is to use something like "clickbait." Sensational headlines like "Before You Renew Amazon Prime, Read This" or "Six Common Reasons You're Gaining Weight" offer teasers that encourage people to click to learn more.

Bad presentations often default to similar tactics. Using superfluous cartoons, pictures of celebrities, or other gimmicks to grab attention and make things seem more relevant.

But while techniques like these can seem alluring, they're not as effective as they might seem.

Clickbait is great for grabbing attention, but it rarely sustains it. While headlines like "Leading Doctor Reveals the Worst Carb You Are Eating" get potential readers to click (which carb is it?! I want to know!), once they start reading the article, they're often disappointed. Sure, the article says something about carbs, but it rarely lives up to the lofty promises sensationalized in the headline. So people open it, skim a couple sentences, and then leave. They never actually read the material.

The same goes for presentation gimmicks. Sometimes they get a laugh or get people to look up from their laptops, but they don't really get people to deeply engage with the material. They grab attention but they don't hold it.

In these, and similar situations, the distinction between attracting and holding attention is key. Senders don't just want recipients to open their emails, they want them to read them. Leaders don't just want employees to attend their presentations, they want them to listen to and internalize what was said. And nonprofits, creators, and content marketers don't just want audiences to glance at their policy briefs, YouTube videos, and white papers, they want them to stick around to consume the content.

To explore what actually holds attention, some colleagues and I analyzed how almost a million people consumed tens of thousands of online articles—not just whether someone clicked on an article but how much of it they read; whether they read the headline and moved on or kept reading for a few paragraphs; whether they skimmed the introduction and left or read the article all the way to the end.

Some topics did a better job of holding readers' attention than others. Articles about sports, for example, tended to engender longer reads than articles about world news, and restaurant reviews tended to hold attention better than articles about education.

But even controlling for *what* articles were about, *how* they were written also mattered. In particular, emotional language increased engagement. The more emotional language an article used, the more likely audiences were to keep reading.

Looking deeper, though, we found that not all emotions had the same effect. While some emotions encouraged sustained attention, others actually discouraged it. People were 30 percent more likely to finish an article that made them feel anxious, for example, than one that made them feel sad.

And to understand why, we have to understand how emotional language shapes the way people see the world.

Take anger and anxiety. Both are negative states. Feeling angry doesn't feel good, and neither does feeling anxious.

But while these two emotions are similar in some ways, one makes us feel much more certain than the other.

Think about the last time you felt angry. An airline lost your bag, a referee blew a call, or a customer service representative hung up on you after you waited on hold.

You probably felt pretty certain. Sure that the airline, referee, or company screwed up and that they were to blame. Indeed, when we're angry, we tend to feel quite confident. Rather than doubt or hesitation, anger often involves righteous indignation, or conviction that we're right and others are wrong.

Anxiety, however, rarely involves such certainty. Think about the last time you felt anxious. Maybe you were worried about whether an airline had lost your bag, nervous that your team might lose, or concerned that you'd be on hold for another thirty minutes. Anxiety is uncertain. It usually involves doubt, ambiguity, or insecurity. Not knowing what will happen and being scared that it might be bad.*

---

* Depending on the situation, sadness can be associated with either certainty or uncertainty. Sometimes we feel sad and certain (e.g., when a dog dies or a friend moves away), and other times we feel sad and uncertain (e.g., when a dog is sick or a friend is considering moving away).

Positive emotions also have different degrees of certainty. Pride is relatively certain, for example, while hope is often uncertain.

	Positive	Negative
Certain	Happiness Pride Excitement	Anger Disgust
Uncertain	Surprise Hope	Anxiety Surprise

It turns out that these differences in certainty have an important impact on sustained attention. Looking across thousands of pieces of content, we found that uncertain emotions encouraged engagement. Language that evoked uncertain emotions (e.g., anxiety and surprise) led readers to keep reading, while language that evoked certain emotions (e.g., disgust) had the opposite effect.

Uncertainty led readers to stick around to resolve what they didn't know. If they weren't sure what would happen next or how something would end, they stayed tuned to find out. Just like not knowing whether it will rain might encourage checking the weather, not knowing what will happen led people to keep reading to resolve the uncertainty.

These findings have some important implications. First, as with many things we've discussed, it's not just what's being talked about, but *how* it's being discussed. Sure, some topics, ideas, presentations, or content may tend to be more naturally interesting than others. People are probably more excited to learn about how they can double their salary than how they can save the company money on airline tickets. Similarly, articles about weight loss secrets may garner more interest than articles about climate change or fiscal policy.

But it's not that some things are inherently interesting and the rest are doomed to fail. By using the right language, the right magic words, we can encourage attention to anything, whether it seems like the most exciting topic or a less exciting one.

This is good news for people and organizations trying to deepen engagement around seemingly less stimulating subject matter. While the area itself might not be the most engaging, using the right language can close the gap. When building presentations, writing emails, or crafting content more generally, picking the right words can make anything more engaging. Style compensates for topic.

Second, emotional language is a powerful tool to increase engagement. Too often, we think facts are the right way to persuade. List attributes to encourage clients to buy, list reasons to encourage colleagues to change their minds, or fill presentations with endless statistics to show something is important. And facts are useful. Sometimes.

But just as often they lull an audience to sleep. Or encourage them to use our presentation as a chance to check social media or catch up on email.

It's tough to persuade people if we can't hold their attention, and that's where emotional language can help. Want to change people's mind about something? Don't just tell them why it's important, use emotional language to get them to care, and pay attention.

Third, while emotional language can deepen engagement, picking the right emotions is key. Sure, some emotions are positive and others are negative, but it's not just about making people feel good and avoid making them feel bad. In fact, making people feel proud or happy may make them less likely to listen to whatever you have to say next.

Because sustaining attention is less about making people feel good or bad, and more about opening up a curiosity gap that makes them want to learn more. Uncertain emotions, or uncertain language more generally, keeps people engaged. If people already know who is going to win the game, there's no reason to watch the rest, but if the outcome is up in the air, they stay tuned to find out.

Making Magic

Most people would like to be more effective communicators. Tell better stories, have better conversations, make better presentations, or build better content. By understanding the value of emotional language, we can do all that and more. To leverage emotions' power:

1. **Highlight the hurdles.** As long as we're already seen as competent, revealing past shortcomings can make people like us more, not less.

2. **Build a roller coaster.** The best stories blend highs and lows. So to increase engagement, know when to go negative. Talking about all the failures along the way makes the successes evermore sweet.

3. **Mix up moments.** The same intuition applies to moments as well. Smooth rides are easy, but not the most engaging, so to hold people's attention, mix it up a bit.

4. **Consider the context.** When trying to persuade, it's not just enough to say something positive. Emotional language can help in hedonic domains like movies and vacations, but backfire in more utilitarian domains like job applications or software.

5. **Connect, then solve.** Solving problems requires understanding people. So rather than jumping into solutions, connect with the person first. Starting with warmer, more emotional language helps

set things up for the more cognitive, problem-solving discussions that come later.

6. **Activate uncertainty.** The right words can make any topic or presentation more captivating. Evoking uncertain emotions (e.g., surprise) will keep people engaged.

By understanding the language of emotions, we can shape how we're perceived, become better storytellers, captivate audiences, and engineer more engaging content.

Next, we examine the last type of magic words, and that is words that suggest similarity.

6

Harness Similarity (and Difference)

Why do some people get promoted while others don't? Why do some songs become hits while others fail? And what drives some books, movies, and TV shows to become blockbusters?

To answer these questions, we first need to start in a very different place. And that is with a bottle of beer.

Early one January, Tim Rooney had his first bottle of Left Hand 400 Pound Monkey. It wasn't his favorite. Okay, but not great; a little sweet, a little buttery, and annoyingly bitter. In sum, a bit weak. At best, 3 out of 5 stars.

In the years since then, Tim has sampled a number of beers. It's hard to know exactly how many, but he's tried at least 4,200 bottles. Because that's how many beers he's rated on RateBeer.com: lagers and ales, pilseners and porters, sours and Stouts. From mass-market brands you can find at your local supermarket (e.g., Michelob Light) to craft breweries that you've probably never heard of before (e.g., Cascade Brewing's Bourbonic Plague and Avery Brewing Company's Rumpkin).

His favorite was Deschutes Brewery's The Abyss (5 stars: "Body is full and extremely thick, oily, soft carbonation, with a long slightly bitter finish. Amazing!"). His least favorite was Black Mountain Brewing Company's Cave Creek Chili Beer (0.5 stars: "I love chili peppers, and I love beer, but this crap is TERRIBLE. Just not a good combo at all. Two sips and drain pour."). In between are thousands of beers described as everything from "lightly sweet" to "clean and crisp with a golden color."

Tim is one of the hundreds of thousands of zythophiles, or beer lovers, who use RateBeer. The site was founded in 2000 as a place for beer drinkers to exchange information and share opinions, and since then, users have provided more than 11 million ratings. Today the site is recognized as one of the most highly touted, in-depth, and accurate sources of beer information.

But in 2013, some scientists from Stanford University became interested in the site for a very different reason. They wanted to study linguistic change.

Groups are in constant flux. New members join, old members leave, and, as a result, things are constantly shifting. A group of coworkers may have lunch together in the conference room, for example, but as stalwarts retire and new employees join, eventually interest may dwindle.

The researchers were interested in such shifts, but in the context of language. How do the words group members use evolve over time? Do new members change their language as they acclimate to the group?

And might these changes provide insights into which users are more likely to stick around long term?

RateBeer provided the perfect testing ground. Each month's reviews served as a snapshot of how people were using language at that point in time. And because many users provided multiple reviews, the researchers could easily track how their language evolved, from the moment they joined the community till whenever they stopped posting.

Take something like a beer's smell. In the site's early years, reviewers tended to use the word "aroma" for these discussions (e.g., "It had a faint aroma of hops."). Eventually, though, they stopped using this term and replaced it with the letter S, short for "smell" (e.g., "It had a faint S of hops.").

The usage of fruit-related words (e.g., "peach" and "pineapple") also changed. Even looking within reviews of the exact same beer, as time passed, reviewers began using more fruity words (e.g., "slight hints of citrus" or "tropical flavor") to describe a beer's taste and feel. The beer itself didn't change, but the way people described it did.

No one sent out a memo telling people to write that way, and there was no meeting where everyone agreed to change their lingo. But over time, the terminology shifted. Like a living organism, the group's language changed.

Individuals' language also shifted. As users spent more time on the site, they started adopting the language of the community. Comparing someone's early reviews to their later ones, for example, showed distinct differences. Not only did people use a lot more beer-related vocabulary, like "carbonation" and "lacing" (the residue left from the foam head), but they used fewer words like "I" or "my." They were less likely to write "I think . . ." or "In my opinion . . ." and more likely to conform to the site's norm of reviews, which read like a list of objective facts.

To provide a more comprehensive analysis, the researchers calculated how similar each user's language was to the rest of the community. How similar the words they used were to the rest of the reviews written on RateBeer at that point in time.

They found that people's behavior on the site could be broken into two distinct stages. When users first joined, they were relatively flexible. They learned the language of the community and started using it themselves, adopting whatever conventions others were using at the time.

But after that initial period of accommodation, users entered a more conservative phase. They stopped adapting new words and phrases and their language calcified. The community and its norms kept moving forward, but older users no longer moved with it.

Language also helped predict how long users kept posting on the site. Some users stayed for years, while others left after a few months. But their words provided a telling sign of what they would end up doing. Users who adopted fewer of the site's linguistic conventions, or had a shorter period of adapting to community language, were more likely to leave. Based on their first few reviews, one could predict how long they would stay engaged.

Their language foretold their future actions, even if they may not have realized it yet themselves.

The first five chapters of this book talked about different types of magic words. Words that activate identity and agency, words that convey confidence, words that ask the right questions, words that communicate concreteness, and words that express emotion.

But to truly understand language, and its impact, we have to put it in context. How the words one person uses relate to the words other people are using.

And that is where the beer study comes in. Because rather than suggesting that some words are good and others are bad, it highlights the importance of *linguistic similarity*. In this case, people whose language matched the group's tended to be more likely to stick around.

Understanding whether people are going to keep contributing to an online community, though, is only one of the many things distance helps explain. And to harness its power we need to know (1) when to signal similarity, (2) when to be different, and (3) how to plot the right progression.

SIGNAL SIMILARITY

Organizational culture has become a hot topic. Building a strong culture, maintaining it, and hiring applicants who fit.

But what *is* organizational culture exactly? Beyond some vague notion of beliefs and values, can it actually be measured? And does fitting in with organizational culture have implications for how well people do at work?

Just like online beer communities have terminology and linguistic norms, so do organizations. Different tribes have different lingo. Startup founders talk about "pivoting," retailers talk about "omnichannel," and Wall Street traders talk about "pikers" and being "junked up."

But beyond slang and terminology, there are other ways organizations or industries use language differently. Some may tend to use shorter, more clipped sentences, while others may use longer ones. Some may use more concrete language while others may talk more abstractly.

To study the link between language and success at work, a team of scientists looked at a data source we don't usually think much about: email.[1] Unlike RateBeer users, employees don't write online reviews. But they do write emails. Lots of them. Emails asking colleagues for information and emails providing feedback on others' work. Emails sharing drafts of presentations and emails scheduling a time to meet with a client. Thousands of notes about every topic imaginable.

Just for fun, take a minute, open your "Sent Items" folder, and scan what's inside. It might seem like normal work and personal stuff. Trivial even. And it often is. But it's not just any work and personal stuff. It's *your* work and personal stuff.

Those notes about the headers on a particular document or what image should go on page 23 of a PowerPoint deck might seem insignificant, but they provide a snapshot of what's going on in your work life. Not only the progression of various projects and decisions, but how you have evolved as a colleague, leader, and potentially even friend. They're pottery shards or remnants of that ancient civilization that is you at the office. And consequently, they provide a lot of information about you and how you have, or haven't, changed over time.

The scientists looked at five years of data, more than 10 million emails sent between hundreds of employees of a midsized firm. Everything Susan in Accounting sent to Tim in HR and everything Lucinda in Sales sent to James in R&D. And rather than looking at how many emails were sent, or who the emails were sent to, the researchers looked at the words each employee used.

But this is where the study gets even more interesting. Because rather than focusing on the content of what employees talked about (e.g., document headers or PowerPoint slides), the researchers zeroed in on something completely different: employee's linguistic style.

When reading an email, talking on the phone, or considering any type of communication, we tend to focus on its content. Take this chapter. If asked to reflect on the language, you'd probably think about the subject matter or topic being discussed. The chapter started out talking about an online beer rating community, for example, before moving into a discussion of email language.

The same can be said for email. If someone asked you to look at your email and report back on the language used, you'd probably focus on the main topics. There were a bunch of emails about this meeting, others about a particular project, and a few regarding that big retirement party you've been planning for a coworker.

All these are examples of content. The subject matter, topic, or substance of what was being discussed.

But while content is clearly important, there's another dimension that often goes unnoticed: *linguistic style*. Consider the phrase "They said to follow up in a couple weeks." The content (following up in a couple weeks) provides a sense of what is happening, but embedded within the content are words like "they," "to," and "a."

These pronouns, articles, and other style words often fade into the background. We often don't even notice that they are there. In fact, even after I mentioned them, you probably had to look closely to find them in the sentences. They're almost invisible. People gloss over them as they jump between the nouns, verbs, and adjectives that make up the linguistic content, or what was said.

But while they're often ignored, style words actually provide a lot of information. Communicators have only so much flexibility in the content they're communicating. If someone asks when a client said to follow up, and the answer is "In a couple weeks," some version of those words is probably needed to communicate the idea.

But *how* we communicate that idea is up to us. We could say, "They said to follow up in a couple weeks," "Following up a couple weeks from now would be good," or any number of variations. And while these differences might seem minor, because they reflect how people communicate, they provide insight into the communicators themselves. Everything from personality and preferences, to how smart people are and whether they are lying.[2]

The researchers analyzed employees' linguistic style. In particular, how similar people's linguistic style was to that of their coworkers

Or, said another way, their cultural fit. Whether employees used language the same way as others around them. Whether someone used personal pronouns (e.g., "we" or "I") when communicating with colleagues who used them a lot or used articles (e.g., "a" or "the") and prepositions (e.g., "in" or "to") to a similar degree as their peers.

The results were remarkable. Similarity shaped success. Employees whose linguistic style was more similar to their coworkers' were three times more likely to be promoted. They received better performance evaluations and higher bonuses.

In some ways, this is great news. If you fit in well at your new job, you're likely to do well.

But what about everybody else? What happens to people who don't fit in?

Indeed, people with a dissimilar linguistic style weren't so fortunate. They were four times more likely to be fired.

So are people who don't fit in from the get-go just destined to fail?

Not quite. Because rather than just studying whether employees fit in initially, the researchers also examined how their fit changed over time. Whether some employees were more adaptable than others.

Similar to the beer community, most new hires adapted quickly. After a year at the firm they had acclimated to the organization's linguistic norms.

Not everyone, however, adapted to the same degree. Some adapted more quickly while others adapted more slowly.

Adaptability, in turn, helped explain success. While successful employees adapted, those who would eventually be fired never did. They started with low cultural fit and slowly declined from there.

Linguistic similarity even helped distinguish between employees who stayed at the firm and those who left to pursue better options. Not because they got fired, but because they were offered something better elsewhere. These folks assimilated early on, but at some point, their language started to diverge. While clearly capable of adapting, eventually they stopped trying, foreshadowing their intention to quit.

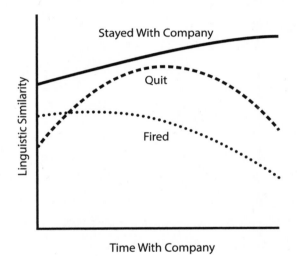

Time With Company

Adaptability ended up being more important than initial fit. People who were a good fit initially did do well, but those who adapted quickly to the changing norms were even more successful. Fit isn't something we have to be born with, we just have to be willing to adapt over time.

The email study highlights the benefits of fitting in. Using similar language can lead to better performance evaluations, higher bonuses, and a greater likelihood of being promoted. And similarity's benefits go far beyond just life at the office. Daters who talk similarly are more likely to go on a second date, students who write similarly are more likely to become friends, and couples who use language more similarly are more likely to be dating three months later.[3]

Using similar language can facilitate conversation, make people feel connected, and increase their perception that they are part of the same tribe. All of which can increase liking, trust, and a variety of positive downstream outcomes.

But is fitting in always a good thing? Or might there be situations where difference is better?

To find out, I had to get into the music business.

DRIVE DIFFERENCE

On a cold fall afternoon, Montero Hill was making music where he always made music: in his bedroom. Well, in the closet of his bedroom. Or in the closet of his grandma's house. Whichever was quieter at the time.

Like many aspiring musicians, the unemployed nineteen-year-old college dropout was trying different things, trying to make a hit. He was pushing his music through the internet full-time, posting songs on SoundCloud and struggling to get traction.

On Halloween, he was scrolling through YouTube looking for beats when he found something that spoke to him. A re-worked sample of a Nine Inch Nails track made by an aspiring producer in the Netherlands—who also made music in his bedroom.

Montero bought the beat for thirty dollars, put down some lyrics, and released a song a few weeks later.

The likelihood that any particular song will becomes a hit is extremely low. And for new artists or those without a record deal that encourages radio airplay, the likelihood is even lower.

There are hundreds of millions of songs on SoundCloud, and hundreds of thousands are added each day. Few are played more than a handful of times, and among those, most are hits by artists who already have a large following.

But this song was different. This song broke the internet.

Montero's (or, as he is now known, Lil Nas X's) "Old Town Road" has been streamed billions of times. It sold more than 10 million units and made *Billboard* history, spending nineteen straight weeks at the top of the charts. It also made Lil Nas X a household name, leading him to be named one of *Time* magazine's most influential people on the internet. Not bad for a kid making music in his bedroom.

But what made "Old Town Road" so successful? And might its success say something deeper about why things catch on?

Industry execs, cultural critics, and consumers alike have long wondered why some songs succeed while others fail. Some tracks get millions of streams, while others barely get listened to. For every "Old Town Road" that burns up the charts, there are thousands, if not tens of thousands, of songs that never get traction.

One possibility is that success is random. That it is luck or chance that a particular song ends up making it. Indeed, even so-called experts are pretty poor at separating the wheat from the chaff. Elvis was told he should go back to driving trucks. The Beatles were told guitar groups were on their way out. Lady Gaga was told her music was too "dance-oriented" to be marketable. Even if some logic exists behind how hits happen, that deeper truth often seems impossible to discern.

To see if there might be something more systematic going on, though a few years ago Grant Packard and I started exploring what makes a hit.[4] Every song is different, but we wondered whether successful songs might have something in common. Specifically, whether they might tend to be similar to, or different from, other songs in their genre. And to measure similarity, we examined the themes each song covered.

For certain songs, the main themes are easy to see. Diana Ross and Lionel Richie's "Endless Love" is clearly a love song. Not only is "love" in the title, but it starts with the phrase "My love," the third line has "love" in it, and the word "love" appears twelve more times throughout the song.

The same goes for songs like Rihanna's "We Found Love," Boyz II Men's "I'll Make Love to You," and Céline Dion's "Because You Loved Me." Their titles and lyrics make it easy to classify them as love songs, and, indeed, they're often listed among the best or most popular love songs of all times.

But other songs are tougher to classify. Natalie Imbruglia's "Torn," for example, is about love and the emotional challenges of a tough breakup. But look for the word "love" in the song, and you won't find it. That word doesn't appear in the title or any of the lyrics. The same goes for other love songs such as Peter, Paul and Mary's "Leaving on a Jet Plane" and No Doubt's "Don't Speak."

Further, while some songs are clearly about love, it's not obvious that all love songs are truly that similar. Elvis Presley's "Can't Help Falling in Love" and Carrie Underwood's "Before He Cheats" both touch on love, but they're clearly not the same. Some love songs (e.g., Katrina & and the Waves' "Walking on Sunshine") are about happy, positive love, some (e.g., Rick Springfield's "Jessie's Girl") are about unrequited love, and some (e.g., Alanis Morissette's "You Oughta Know") are about anger toward an ex.

Saying that these songs are about the same thing would be like saying that chocolate cake and crab cakes are the same. Sure, they both include the word "cake," but they're pretty different.

Outside of love songs, things get even tougher. What's the Beatles' "Hey Jude" about? Or Prince's "When Doves Cry"? Different people tend to have very different answers. Some people think that Bruce Springsteen's "Born in the U.S.A." is about patriotism and American pride, for example, but it's actually about how shamefully the United States treated Vietnam War veterans.

All this is to say that people's perceptions may not be the most reliable indicator of the main themes of a song. So rather than have people do it, we asked a computer for help.

Imagine being a high school student who just moved to a new city. You don't know anyone at your new school or who is friends with whom, so you need to learn through observation. If you repeatedly see Danny and Eric together, for example, you'd assume they are friends. If one of them often hangs out with Lucy, or they often all hang out together, you'd probably assume they're all part of the same group.

Along these lines, you might create other groupings based on who hangs out together. The jocks, geeks, gamers, and the theater kids.

These groups are amorphous and informal, but they shed light on how people are organized. First, not everyone in the group hangs out together simultaneously. You might see two gamers talking before school, for example, and later see two different gamers grabbing lunch. But by seeing different pairs or subsets of them together often enough, you can get a sense of who belongs to the larger group.

Second, some people are more strongly tied to particular groups than others. Lucy might often be there when the jocks hang out, for example, but Eric might not be. He might be there only 20 percent of the time.

The same ideas can be applied to words. Just as we might infer group membership by who hangs out with whom, a statistical approach called topic modeling uses word co-occurrence to infer underlying topics or themes.[5]

If songs that include the word "love" often include the words "feel" and "heart," for example, all those words might be grouped together. Similarly, if words such as "bounce" and "clap" or "jump" and "shake" often appear together, they might be grouped together as well. By looking across songs (or any other passages of text), and the words that appear in them, topic modeling groups words together based on how frequently they co-occur.

Note that this approach doesn't require specifying the groups in advance. Rather than deciding that there must be some love songs and sorting each song based on whether it falls into that group or not, topic modeling lets the topics (e.g., love) emerge from the data. The patterns of words across songs determine what the groups are and how many of them there should be. There might be two or three different types of love, for example, or themes such as family or technology that listeners might not even realize are there. But by looking across songs and the words that appear in them, the main themes emerge.

In our case, running this approach across thousands of songs identified the main themes or topics that appear in song lyrics. Not surprisingly, love was a key theme. In addition to fiery love (e.g., words like "love," "fire," and "burn"), for example, there was also uncertain love (e.g., words like "love," "need," and "never").

But there were other themes as well. Body movement (e.g., "bounce," "jump," and "shake"), dance moves (e.g., "bop," "twerk," and "mash"), and girls and cars (e.g., "girl," "road," "kiss," and "car"), among others.

Most songs mixed multiple themes. Whitney Houston's "I Wanna Dance with Somebody (Who Loves Me)" clearly talks about dancing,

Topic	Example topic words
Anger and violence	bad, dead, hate, kill, slay
Body movement	body, bounce, clap, jump, shake
Dance moves	bop, dab, mash, nae, twerk
Family	American, boy, daddy, mamma, whoa
Fiery love	burn, feel, fire, heart, love
Girls and cars	car, drive, girl, kiss, road
Positivity	feel, like, mmm, oh, yeah
Spiritual	believe, grace, lord, one, soul
Street cred	ass, bitch, dope, rich, street
Uncertain love	ain't, can't, love, need, never

but it's also a love song. Other songs focused on both family and positivity. Just as high school students can be both jocks and gamers or theater kids and class clowns, songs can be about multiple topics, some of them more strongly than others.

By identifying how often words from each theme appeared in each song, we quantified how much each song dealt with each theme. Then, by averaging across all songs in a genre, we could get a sense of what each genre tended to talk about.

Country songs, for example, sang a lot about girls and cars (about 40 percent of their lyrics were about that topic) but not so much about body movement. Rap songs talked a lot about street cred and not so much about love. Dance and rock songs talked more about fiery love, while pop songs talked more about uncertain love.

Finally, we analyzed the link between atypicality and success. Whether popular songs tended to talk about similar (or different) things from other songs in their genres.

Sure, country songs tend to sing a lot about girls and cars, but any individual song may adhere more or less to the norm. It may focus a lot on that topic or not as much. Similarly, most rock songs talk about fiery love, but others are more about uncertain love or dance moves. By comparing each song with others in its genre, we could get a sense of how typical it was and whether that fact contributed at all to how popular it had become.

It turned out that atypical songs were more successful. A country song about girls and cars, for example, tended to do pretty well, but one that was about more atypical themes like dance moves or street cred was even more likely to be a hit. The more differentiated a song's lyrics were from its genre, the more popular it tended to be.

And it wasn't just because famous artists tend to use more atypical lyrics or that atypical songs get more airplay. Even controlling for those aspects, and dozens of other potentially confounding factors, atypical songs still sold more copies and generated more streams.

In fact, even looking at cases where the same song charted in two different genres, that song ended up being more popular on the chart where it was more atypical. The artist, lyrics, and everything else remained the same, but in the genre where the lyrics were more unusual, the song did better.[*]

Difference drove success.

Returning to Lil Nas X's chart-topping hit, understanding the link between atypicality and success helps explain why "Old Town Road" became so successful.

The song has lots of country elements. It starts with the twang of a

---

[*] One might wonder whether atypical songs were more popular because we only looked at songs that are at least somewhat successful. Maybe unpopular failures also tend to be different from the norm. To test this possibility, we looked at a matched control group of non-hits. For each song that made the chart, we randomly selected another song by the same artists from the same album that never made the charts. Compared to hits, though, these matched non-hits were more typical, underscoring the notion that atypicality boosts success.

banjo instrumental, and its first lyrics are about a quintessential country thing, riding horses ("Yeah, I'm gonna take my horse to the old town road/I'm gonna ride 'til I can't no more").

Listen further, and it's full of country tropes, everything from cowboy boots and hats to Wrangler jeans and bull riding. Lil Nas X himself indicated that the tune was country when he released it, the country legend Billy Ray Cyrus appears on the remix, and when the song debuted on the *Billboard* charts, it appeared on the "Hot Country Songs" list.

But listen more closely, and it becomes clear that "Old Town Road" is far from the typical country tune. In addition to horses and cowboy boots, it talks about Porsches, being lean, and booties. The remix with Billy Ray mentions Maseratis and Fendi sports bras. And that cowboy hat? Rather than being a Stetson, it's from Gucci.

The same goes for the music. Sure, there's a banjo, but there are also 808s and bass throughout—features more common in hip-hop than in country. Indeed, though "Old Town Road" first appeared on the *Billboard* country chart, it moved to the "Hot Rap Songs" chart the following week.

Call it country trap, hick-hop, or anything else you want, but "Old Town Road" is clearly atypical. This genre-flouting, boundary-busting tune defies classification. Too rap to be a country tune and too country to be a rap song, it blends conventions to create something new and different.

But while the song itself is atypical, the reason for its success was far from it. In fact, its success was downright predictable. Its unusual nature was exactly why it became a hit.*

---

* While atypical songs were more popular, one could argue that having more typical musical features might help localize songs within their genre. The plucked strings that kick off Old Town Road, for example, immediately evoke a country song. Similar sounds and unusual lyrics may provide the optimal mix of new and old. Similar enough to evoke the warm glow of familiarity, but different enough to feel exciting and novel.

WHEN SIMILARITY IS GOOD AND
DIFFERENCE IS BETTER

The music study's results are interesting, but juxtaposed with the email study, they raise some important questions. Using similar language seems to pay off at the office, but using different language makes songs more successful. So when is similarity good and when is difference better?

It's easy to focus on something specific to the particular domains. Email language might be more formal, for example, while music is more expressive. Email tends to be written for a small audience, while music is written for a larger one.

But at its core, the difference is really about what similarity and difference evoke or connote, and which is better in the particular context being considered.

Linguistic similarity has a number of benefits. Using similar language often requires listening to what someone else said, so, not surprisingly, it is associated with everything from better dates to more successful negotiations.[6] As noted, such coordination can make people feel that they're on the same team or part of the same tribe, which can boost liking, trust, and affiliation. Indeed, friends tend to use language similarly, and people who use language similarly are more likely to become friends. Just like sharing a birthday or attending the same high school, using language similarly can serve as a signal that two people have something in common or are on the same page.

That said, there are also benefits to differentiation. Just as having the same conversation over and over again would quickly get tedious, eventually people tire of hearing the same song. They have an ingrained drive for novelty and stimulation and value new things, in part, because they satisfy those needs. Rather than doing the same thing again and again, they look for new things that provide variety and excitement.

Differentiation is also linked to creativity and memorability. Creative people's thoughts tend to jump among different ideas, and slogans and movie quotes that are phrased more distinctively (e.g., "May the Force be with you" or "Frankly, Scarlett, I don't give a damn") are easier to remember.[7]

Overall, then, similarity and difference can both be good and bad. Similarity feels familiar and safe but can also be boring. Difference can be exciting and stimulating but can also be risky.

Consequently, whether similarity or difference is better depends on what is valued in a particular context.

In most offices, fitting in is important. Sure, companies say they want innovation and creativity, but the main thing they want is for employees to follow directions and get their work done. They want people who can assimilate and be good members of the group, and group-consistent language provides a useful signal. There may be times when difference is valued, but in general, similarity is preferred.

When considering new music, however, people like stimulation, so difference is better. Atypical movies are also more successful, and the same may be true for other cultural products, like musicals. One reason *Hamilton* was such a big hit was that its style diverged from what theatergoers were used to.

In fact, though atypical songs are generally more popular, the pattern for pop music is the reverse. This makes a lot of sense. Pop music, almost by definition, is about being similar rather than different. Often derided for being bland or formulaic, it's designed to be mainstream rather than avant-garde. Not surprisingly, then, in a domain in which familiarity is valued, similar songs are more successful.

Are you working in a domain where creativity, innovation, or stimulation is valued? Linguistic differentiation may be beneficial. Are you doing a job where familiarity, fitting in, and safety are desired? Linguistic similarity may be better.

WHICH IS MOST SIMILAR TO A GRAPEFRUIT?

The beer, email, and music studies all examined similarity between things: between users and the community, people and their colleagues, songs and their genres.

But it turns out that similarity also matters in a different way, and that is between pieces or parts of the same thing (i.e., the sections of a book).

Even if you haven't heard of *The Girl with the Dragon Tattoo*, you probably know someone who has. The psychological thriller was the first book in the Swedish author Stieg Larsson's Millennium series and introduced the world to its heroine, Lisbeth Salander, a brilliant but deeply troubled computer hacker. Originally published in Sweden, the novel achieved great acclaim there before being translated throughout the world. The series has sold more than 100 million copies and has been listed as one of the top hundred books of the twenty-first century.

Many things obviously contribute to a hit book's success. The topic has to be interesting, the characters have to be engaging, and the plot has to be good. But what makes a plot, well, good?

The emotional trajectories we talked about in chapter 5 provide some insight, but there's more than just that going on.

Reviewers of books such as *The Girl with the Dragon Tattoo* often use the same phrases: "The story moved quickly," "It was gripping, and the plot never dragged," "It moved fast and kept me engaged." Indeed, people often mention a fast-moving plot as part of why they liked what they read. But what does it mean for a plot to be fast moving? And is it always better for a plot to move quickly?

To answer this question, we first need to understand the relationship, or similarity, between words.

Which is most similar to a grapefruit? A kiwi, an orange, or a tiger?

This seems like an easy question to answer. And if you're a person, or at least a person over the age of three, the answer is pretty obvious. (It's an orange.)

But to judge the similarity of thousands of words and do so quickly, you need a computer. And it turns out that questions like this can be surprisingly difficult for computers to answer right.

Machine learning is based on the notion that computers can learn from data. They can take available information, identify patterns, and even make decisions, all with minimal or even no human intervention.

Think about Amazon or Netflix recommendations. They aren't made by people or elves who scour the web for information, they're made by machines. Algorithms look at what you have viewed or purchased and what others have viewed or purchased and use the data to make an educated guess about what else you might like.

Recently bought a shirt for work or a coffee maker for the kitchen? Amazon might suggest similar shirts or new kitchen gadgets that other people who bought these products tend to like. Recently watched *The Bourne Identity*? Netflix might suggest a James Bond movie or some other action film.

To make such suggestions, particularly accurate ones, the algorithm has to observe relationships. People who bought X tend to like Y, so if you bought X, Y is probably a decent suggestion.

Autocomplete, or predictive text, on your phone works similarly. Type the letter d, and your phone might suggest the word "do." Accept or write that word, and it might then suggest a series of words such as "we," "need," "more," and "milk." The algorithm uses the words and phrases you (and others) have written to make educated guesses about what you want to say.

Unlike recommendations, though, deciding whether a kiwi or an orange is more similar to a grapefruit can be tough for a computer because their relationships aren't easy to observe. People don't buy grapefruit on Amazon, and although they buy them at the supermarket, that data wouldn't be that useful, either. Some people buy grapefruits, some buy kiwis, and some buy oranges, but buying patterns don't provide much insight into the similarities between the items. People who buy grapefruit may also buy bread, fish, or any number of other things, so the fact that things are frequently bought together doesn't mean much. In fact, grapefruit might often be purchased with cottage cheese, but the two aren't that similar.

But while purchase data aren't that helpful for inferring similarity between objects, everyday language data are.

Each day, billions of people write trillions of words on the internet. News articles are written, online reviews are posted, and information is updated. Each article or review might not seem that important by itself, but together they provide a comprehensive view of the relationship between various concepts and ideas.

Take a sentence such as "The doctor came into the operating room and put on gloves." On the surface, it might seem simple, but to a computer trying to learn the relationship between different words and concepts, it provides many beneficial crumbs of information. It suggests that something called a "doctor" goes into something called an "operating room" and puts on something called "gloves."

Similar to the approach we used to identify song themes, looking across many sentences that use similar words starts to provide a sense of how different words, concepts, or ideas relate. If "doctors" are often going into and out of "operating rooms," using "gloves," or talking to "patients," one can start to get a sense of what a "doctor" is and does.

This is how children learn. The first time a fifteen-month-old sees you point to the thing in the middle of your face and say "nose," she has no idea what you're talking about. To her, a nose is just as novel and foreign as democracy or antidisestablishmentarianism. But by repeatedly hearing you say "nose" as you point to yours, hers, or a picture of one in a book, she eventually learns what a nose is.

Machines learn the same way. By ingesting all the articles on Wikipedia, for example, or everything that appears on Google News, computers can start to learn what different words mean and how they are related.

If "dogs" are often talked about as being "friendly," for example, readers (and machines) may start to associate those two concepts and treat them as more related. Similarly, if "cats" are often talked about as "aloof," it can strengthen the link between those two concepts.

Words don't even have to co-occur for these links to form. If phrases such as "Dogs are animals" and "Animals are friendly" both appear often enough, the computer associates "dog" and "friendly" even if dogs are not often explicitly talked about as friendly.

The British linguist J. R. Firth once noted, "You shall know a word by the company it keeps." Said another way, you can learn a lot about what words mean and the relationships among them by looking at the contexts they show up in and the words that surround them. Just as we infer that people who hang out together frequently are more likely to be friends, words that show up near one another are more likely to be connected in some way.

Building on this idea, a technique called *word embedding* uses the relationships among words to plot them on a multidimensional space. When moving into a new house or apartment and putting things away in the kitchen, people tend to put related things together: the spoons go into the silverware drawer, the vegetables go into the fridge, and the cleaning chemicals go under the sink.

Word embedding does something similar with words: the more related words are to one another, the closer together they are positioned. The words "dog" and "cat" are probably pretty close together, for example, because they are both animals and pets. But based on their associations, the word "dog" might be closer to the word "friendly," whereas the word "cat" would be closer to the word "aloof."

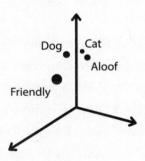

Rather than using just two or three dimensions, this technique often uses hundreds of dimensions.

And because related words appear closer together, the similarity between words can be measured by the distance between them. The word "grapefruit," for example, is closer to the word "orange" than it is to "kiwi," indicating that they are more similar. And all of these fruit words, not surprisingly, are pretty far from the word "tiger."

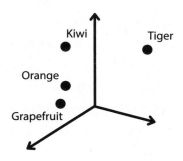

PLOT THE RIGHT PROGRESSION

Word embeddings are remarkable. And as we'll talk about in the last chapter, they can be used to study everything from gender bias and racism to the evolution of thought.

But to study whether books and movies are more successful when the plot moves faster, some colleagues and I decided to apply the same underlying idea to larger chunks of text (sentences or paragraphs). Just as two words can be more or less similar or related to each other, two parts of a book, movie, or any other piece of content can also be more or less similar.

To understand how this works, think about an earth science textbook one might have studied in high school. There are chapters on the earth's crust, earthquakes, weather, and even the solar system.

Take the first part of any chapter, say on earthquakes, and it's quite related to the next part of that chapter. The chapter might start by defining an earthquake and then move to what causes one, both of which involve similar words, phrases, and concepts (e.g., "earthquake," "fault," and "plate tectonics").

But while consecutive parts of a chapter are quite similar, the farther apart two parts of a textbook are, the less related they tend to be. The earthquake chapter, for example, uses very different concepts, terms, and ideas than the chapter on the solar system does.

This same idea can be applied to novels, movies, or any other text. A scene about a wedding, for example, is probably pretty similar to another scene about that same wedding. The characters are the same, the setting is the same, and people are likely doing related things.

That wedding scene, however, is probably less similar to a scene about an alien invasion, scuba diving, or fixing a car. Even if the people involved were the same, the places, items, and things involved would be quite different.

Importantly, though consecutive pieces of a book or movie are usually at least somewhat related, *how* related they are can vary; they might be quite similar or more different.

By measuring the distance between consecutive pieces of a story, we determined how quickly it was moving.[8] If a story jumped from talking about the first part of a wedding to talking about an alien invasion, for example, the plot moved faster than a story that went from the first part of a wedding to the second. Just as one car is going faster than another if it

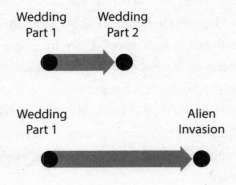

travels a greater distance in the same amount of time, stories move faster when they jump between less related ideas.

Then, to examine the relationship between speed and success, we analyzed tens of thousands of books, movies, and TV shows, everything from classics by Charles Dickens and Jack Kerouac to more recent books such as *High Fidelity* by Nick Hornby and *Safe Harbor* by Danielle Steel, as well as movies such as *Star Wars* and *Pulp Fiction* and shows such as *I Love Lucy*, *South Park*, and *Friday Night Lights*.

Overall, we found that speed was good. Books, movies, and TV shows with faster plot progression were liked more than their slower-moving counterparts.

Just as atypical lyrics make songs more interesting to listen to, a faster plot progression makes a story more stimulating. Rather than just plodding along, moving faster between more differentiated topics and ideas is more exciting, which leads audiences to react more favorably.

In addition, we found that within stories, there were times when plots should move faster and times when they should move more slowly.[9]

At the beginning of a book or movie, the canvas is blank. An audience doesn't know who the characters are, what the setting is, or how everything relates. So the beginning of a story sets the stage, building a base or jumping-off point for the rest of the narrative.

Starting slowly is key. It takes time for the audience members to digest the characters, their relationships, and everything else, so a plot that moves too quickly at the outset may confuse them. In a relay race, if the second runner dashes off too quickly, the first runner may never be able to catch up and hand off the baton. The same goes for a story: if the plot moves too fast right off the bat, the audience may get left in the dust.

And that was exactly what we found: early on, speed was detrimental. Audiences reacted more favorably to stories that moved more slowly initially.

Indeed, rather than moving quickly, famous folktales and children's stories often start by repeating a similar concept. In "The Three Little Pigs," for example, the first pig builds his house of straw, and the wolf blows it down. Then something very similar happens to a second pig.

The same goes for jokes. Comedy often follows a rule of three, or comic triple, in which similar things happen to multiple people. A priest walks into a bar, and something happens. Then a nun walks into the bar, and the same thing happens.

But once similarity has helped lay the groundwork, the story must advance. If the exact same thing happened to a third pig or a rabbi who walked into the bar, the story or joke would quickly get boring. So although similarity helps set the stage and build expectations, once the audience has met the characters and understand the context, it's time for things to pick up.

Indeed, as stories advance, the effect of speed reverses. Though audiences liked stories that moved slowly initially, eventually a faster plot progression was preferred, so much so that toward the end of stories, those that moved faster were liked more.

The speed of stories matters, but whether faster or slower is better depends on the point in the narrative. The best plots start slowly, but once everyone is on board, they pick up steam, building excitement and engagement along the way.

Taken together, these findings have important implications for everything from telling stories to communicating more generally. If the goal is to entertain, speed is good. Moving faster helps keep an audience stimulated and engaged. But the beginning of a piece should be slower to make sure everyone is on board, and then the story can move more quickly as things progress.

If the goal is to inform, however, a different trajectory may be better. Indeed, when we looked at the success of academic papers, which are more about informing than about entertaining, speed was detrimental. Though moving more quickly among related ideas makes content more stimulating, it's also more difficult to follow. So particularly when presenting complex ideas, if your goal is to inform, slow may be the way to go.*

---

* We also measured stories' broader progression. People talk about stories "covering a lot of ground" or "going in circles," and the former can be described as a story's volume, while the latter can be described as it's circuitousness.

In the case of volume, for example, running four miles in forty minutes could mean four times around a mile track or covering more ground by running once around a four-mile loop. The latter covers more ground.

The same holds for stories or narratives. Some cover a lot of ground, traversing a wide range of disparate themes that are quite distant from one another. Others are more localized, dwelling on a smaller set of related ideas. To capture this, we wrapped the set of points in each story in shrink wrap and measured the volume inside.

Volume helped further explain success. Covering a lot of ground was fine for movies, for example, but hurt TV shows. This may be driven by what audiences look for when they consume different mediums. While people who watch movies are often looking for an experience, to think differently, or be transported into a different world, TV shows are often consumed more as a quick diversion. Consequently, covering too many disparate ideas may make things overly confusing and reduce enjoyment.

We also measured circuitousness, or whether stories took a more direct or indirect route. While going in circles might seem like a bad thing, that wasn't always the case. Circuitousness actually helped academic papers. Rather than presenting key concepts only once, presenting them repeatedly, with deepening layers of complexity or in different applications can help people more deeply understand key concepts and increases learning.

Making Magic

We're often so focused on *what* we want to communicate that we don't think a lot about *how* we're communicating it. And linguistic similarity can be even tougher to perceive.

But that doesn't mean it doesn't matter, because similarity shapes everything from who is promoted and fired to whether songs, books, and movies become hits. To leverage its value:

1. **Signal similarity.** When familiarity is useful or fitting in is the goal, similar language can help. Paying more attention to how our colleagues are using words, for example, and adopting some of their mannerisms should help us thrive at the office.

2. **Drive difference.** But similarity isn't always good; there are also benefits to differentiation, particularly if you're doing a job in which creativity, innovation, or stimulation is valued, standing out might be better.

3. **Plot the right progression.** Further, when drafting presentations, writing stories, or crafting certain types of content, think about the progression of ideas. Start slowly to make sure the audience is on board before speeding up to increase excitement, particularly when entertainment is the goal. But if your goal is to

inform, slowing down but covering more ground is the better way to go.

By beginning to understand and notice linguistic similarity, we can communicate more effectively, craft better content, and gain more insight into why some things succeed and others fail.

7

What Language Reveals

On December 13, 1727, a play premiered at the Theatre Royal in London. Called *Double Falsehood*, it mixed tragedy and comedy and was written by the playwright Lewis Theobald. It centered on the story of two young women, one highborn and the other of lowly origin, and two men, one honorable and one villainous, and explored entangled relationships, family dynamics, confrontation, and reconciliation.

What was most intriguing about the play, though, was its provenance. The title page claimed that the play had originally been written by none other than William Shakespeare. Theobald said that he had found an undiscovered Shakespearean manuscript that he had painstakingly restored into the newly presented play.

But was the play actually written by Shakespeare? And given that

Shakespeare had been dead for more than a hundred years, how could anyone tell for sure?

FORENSIC LINGUISTICS

Ask people to list the greatest playwrights in history, and the same names tend to come up. Oscar Wilde wrote *The Importance of Being Earnest* and *The Picture of Dorian Gray* and is one of the most popular writers of all time. Tennessee Williams is known for plays such as *A Streetcar Named Desire* and *Cat on a Hot Tin Roof*, and Arthur Miller penned American classics such as *Death of a Salesman* and *The Crucible*.

One name, however, usually appears at the top: Shakespeare. Often called England's national poet, the "Bard of Avon" is widely regarded as the greatest writer in the English language. He is the genius behind comedies such as *A Midsummer Night's Dream* and *The Merchant of Venice* and tragedies such as *Romeo and Juliet* and *Macbeth*, and his plays have been translated into every major language. His work is performed more often than that of any other playwright and is a staple of theaters around the world.

Consistent with this fame, one would expect there to be an easily accessible list of his work. After all, look up Oscar Wilde, Tennessee Williams, or Arthur Miller, and you can find a decisive inventory of everything they've written.

With Shakespeare, though, it's a bit more complicated. Written works weren't protected by copyright at the time, so he didn't distribute scripts of his plays for fear that others would steal them. That led to bootleg versions based on people's memories of what Shakespeare had written.

Further, he didn't publish a formal catalog of his plays before he died, exacerbating the confusion. Indeed, when listing the number of plays Shakespeare wrote, many sources cite "approximately" thirty-nine dramatic works, with the exact number unclear.

One such contested work is *Double Falsehood*. Theobald's claim that it was written by Shakespeare was plausible. After all, Theobald was an avid collector of manuscripts and had published extensively on Shakespeare's work, so he might have discovered an unpublished gem.

But Theobald's original manuscripts were lost in a library fire, making the veracity of the claim hard to verify. Further, given Shakespeare's prominence, many observers were skeptical. They suggested that Theobald was a fraudster trying to pass off work by a lesser-known playwright as authored by Shakespeare to garner attention and sell tickets.

In the centuries that followed, the authorship of the play remained hotly debated. Some scholars offered evidence that the play was written by Shakespeare, while others suggested that the play was written by Theobald. To make matters more complex, a similarly themed play was actually presented in London 150 years earlier, attributed to Shakespeare and a coauthor of his named John Fletcher.

So who wrote the play? Shakespeare, Theobald, Fletcher, or some mix? With the potential authors long deceased, it seemed like the question would never be resolved.

In 2015, though, some behavioral scientists figured out how to solve the puzzle.[1] They didn't sift through historical documents or consult archives. They didn't talk to Shakespeare scholars or pore over specific words or turns of phrase. In fact, they didn't even read *Double Falsehood* to draw their conclusions.

All they did was run the play through a computer.

Imagine you wanted to teach a toddler to recognize different animals. Cows, chickens, goats, and other creatures you might expect to find on a farm.

To start, you might show them a picture of a cow and say the word "cow" a few times. Then, you might show them a picture of a chicken and say the word "chicken." And finally you might repeat the process for a picture of a goat.

One time through, though, probably won't be enough. After all, if a fifteen-month-old has never seen a cow before, they're probably not going to be able to recognize one right away.

So you'd probably have to practice a bit. You'd go through one book with pictures of farm animals, repeat the process a few times, and then maybe switch to another book. You'd show them a few different cows, in a few different poses, all the while saying the word "cow" to encourage them to make the connection.

Eventually, by repeatedly pairing the word "cow" with pictures of large, stocky, four-legged creatures covered in black and white, toddlers get the idea. They realize that a cow isn't just one picture in one book, it's something more. They're able to identify different cows in different books as the same thing and may even be able to recognize new pictures of animals as cows, even in books they've never seen before.

Said simply, they've learned the concept of a cow.

Identifying whether something is a cow or not is an example of classification, and machines can be trained to do it as well. By giving an algorithm a set of pictures and attaching labels to different items (e.g., this one is a cow and this other one isn't), it can start to learn to differentiate. Then, when it's shown a picture of a cow, even one it's never seen before, it can use what it has learned from the other images to correctly categorize whether this new thing is a cow or not.

Texts can be classified in a similar manner. By being trained on relevant examples, algorithms can learn to identify hate speech on social media or determine which section of the newspaper a given article should fall into.

The researchers used a similar approach to determine who had written *Double Falsehood*. They identified every play known to have been written by each of the potential authors. Then they ran each one through text analysis software to identify how many words from each play appeared in hundreds of different categories. How many pronouns (e.g., "I" and "you") each play used, for example, whether it used a lot of words related to emotion, and whether it tended to use longer words or shorter ones.

While not every play by a given playwright was identical on these dimensions, by looking across dozens of plays, the scientists could begin to identify a linguistic signature for each person. Then, by comparing those signatures to the language used in *Double Falsehood*, they could determine who had written it.

The analysis suggested that *Double Falsehood* was no forgery. The first three acts were clearly written by Shakespeare, and the last couple most likely by Shakespeare's previous coauthor John Fletcher. And consistent with his reputation for having a heavy editorial hand, the text of the play revealed traces of Theobald's signature as well.

Two behavioral scientists had solved a centuries-old literary mystery without ever having to read the play.

WHAT LANGUAGE REVEALS

The first six chapters of this book focused on language's impact. How we can use magic words, phrases, and linguistic styles to be happier, healthier, and more successful. How language influences colleagues, friends, customers, and clients.

As the case of *Double Falsehood* illustrates, though, language serves a dual role. Words not only influence and affect the people who listen to or read them, they also *reflect* and *reveal* things about the person (or people) who created them.

Shakespeare tended to use relatively few words related to emotion, for example, while Theobald used many of them. Theobald tended to use lots of prepositions (e.g., "of," "in," and "from") and articles (e.g., "the" and "an"), while Fletcher tended to use lots of auxiliary verbs and adverbs. Different writers tend to write in different ways.

In this way, language is like a fingerprint. It leaves behind traces or signals of the person or people who created it.

Further, because similar people often use language similarly, we can learn a lot about who someone is from the language he or she leaves behind. Older people talk differently from younger ones, Democrats talk differently from Republicans, and introverts talk differently from extroverts.[2] They don't use completely different words, and there is certainly some overlap, but knowing what someone said can help accurately predict their age, political views, and personality.

And the predictive value of language doesn't stop there. You can predict whether someone is lying based on the words they use and whether students will do well in college based on the words in their application essay.[3] You can predict whether someone will get postpartum depression based on her Facebook posts[4] and whether a romantic couple is about to go through a breakup based on their social media posts (even ones that have nothing to do with relationships).[5]

People use language to express themselves, communicate with others, and achieve desired goals, and as a result, the language they use can tell us a lot about who they are, how they are feeling, and what they might do in the future. Even if people aren't communicating strategically or consciously trying to speak one way or another, just like Shakespeare and Theobald, the words they use provide telltale signals of all sorts of interesting and important things.

Like how likely they are to default on a bank loan.

PREDICTING THE FUTURE

Imagine that you're considering lending money to one of two strangers. Each is asking for $2,000 to fix their roof, and their demographics and financial characteristics are identical. They're the same age, race, and gender, live in the same area of the country, and have the same level of income and credit score. In fact, the only difference between them is the words they used when asking for the loan.

Person 1	Person 2
I am a hardworking person, married for 25 years, and have two wonderful boys. Please let me explain why I need help. I would use the $2,000 loan to fix our roof. Thank you, God bless you, and I promise to pay you back.	While the past year in our new place has been more than great, the roof is now leaking, and I need to borrow $2,000 to cover the cost of the repair. I pay all bills (e.g., car loans, cable, utilities) on time.

Which of these people do you think is more likely to pay the money back?

When deciding whether to loan someone money, lenders often focus on the prospective borrower's ability to repay. But while this seems like a simple question, answering it often ends up being quite complex. Loans take a long time to be repaid and many unforeseen circumstances can arise over time. Consequently, banks and other financial institutions often use thousands of data points to estimate the risk of issuing the loan.

The most basic category is the prospective borrower's financial strength. Credit history tracks how many lines of credit (e.g., mortgages, loans, and credit card accounts) someone has taken out, whether he pays his bills on time, and whether he's had any accounts go to collection. A FICO score based on his credit history, income level, and debt is also used. Someone who is already overleveraged, for example, or has filed for bankruptcy in the past may seem like a greater risk to default and fail to repay the loan.

Beyond financial strength, demographics may play a role. Though the Equal Credit Opportunity and Fair Housing Acts prohibit demographic variables such as race and gender from being used directly in loan decisions, some borrowers may rely on correlated factors to help make decisions.

Finally, aspects of the loan itself come into play: the more money requested or the higher the interest rate, the greater the likelihood of default may be.

That said, though all this information can help predict risk, it's not perfectly diagnostic. A credit score, for example, provides a snapshot of what happened in the past, but often misses important factors such as health status and length of employment, which are more forward looking. Personality and emotional state also drive financial behavior but are not captured by purely financial metrics.

Might the words people use provide additional insight?

Crowdfunding and peer-to-peer lending platforms play a key role in today's loan marketplace. Rather than asking a large bank for a loan, consumers can post what they need, and individual investors or potential lenders can decide whom to fund. Investors can often get higher returns than they would for other types of investments and borrowers often get lower interest rates than they might with a traditional bank. Prosper, for example, has enabled more than a million people to get more than $18 billion in loans for everything from paying off college loans to improving their home.

In addition to providing the usual quantitative information (e.g., loan amount and credit score), though, potential borrowers also usually provide a brief blurb. A short description of what they are using the money for and why a lender should choose them. One person might note that they're expanding their business and need the money to buy more product. Another might say that they need money to fix their roof or buy more supplies for their classroom.

Beyond the reason for their request, the language people use also varies. The two people asking for money to fix their roofs in the example above used very different words to do so. One talked about how they are a "hardworking person," while the other noted that they "pay all bills . . . on time." One talked about their family ("married for 25 years, and have two wonderful boys"), while the other did not.

It's easy to see these descriptions as unverifiable "cheap talk." After all, just because someone says they'll "definitely repay the loan" doesn't guarantee that they will. Similarly, someone can say they are trustworthy and dependable even if they are not.

But to find out whether this seemingly idle chatter might shed light on which borrowers default, researchers analyzed more than 120,000 loans requests.[6] In addition to financial information and demographic information (e.g., geographic location, gender, and age), they also analyzed the text would-be borrowers provided in their loan application. Everything from potentially relevant things like how they said the money would be used (i.e., fix a roof or buy more business supplies) to seemingly less relevant things like whether they mentioned their family or religion.

Not surprisingly, financial and demographic information did a pretty good job. Using these variables alone, one could predict who would default with decent accuracy.

But analyzing the text improved things even further. Incorporating what people happened to write in their description significantly increased predictive accuracy. Compared to only using financial and demographic information, incorporating textual information would increase lenders' return on investment by almost 6 percent.

In fact, just the text itself was nearly as predictive as the usual financial and demographic information that banks might use. While borrowers clearly wanted to get funded, without realizing it, the words they used shed light on whether they would actually end up paying the loan back.

The researchers also identified which words or phrases best differentiated between repayers and defaulters. Repayers were more likely to use words and phrases related to their financial situation (e.g., "interest" and "tax") or improvements in financial ability (e.g., "graduate" and "promote"). They also used words and phrases that indicated their financial literacy (e.g., "reinvest" and "minimum payment") and were more likely to discuss topics such as employment and school, interest rate reductions, and monthly payments.

Defaulters, on the other hand, used distinctly different language. They were more likely to mention words or phrases related to financial hardships (e.g., "payday loan" or "refinance"), for example, or hardship more generally (e.g., "stress" or "divorce"), as well as words and phrases that tried to explain their situation (e.g., "explain why") or discuss their work state (e.g., "hard work" or "worker"). Similarly, they were more likely to plead for help (e.g., "need help" or "please help") or touch on religion.

In fact, while people who used the word "reinvest" were almost 5 times more likely to repay their loan in full, those who used the word "God" were almost 2 times more likely to default.

In other cases, repayers and defaulters talked about similar topics but in different ways. Both used time-related words, for example, but defaulters seemed to focus more on the near term (e.g., the next month) while repayers focused on the longer term (e.g., the next year). Similarly, both talked about people, but while repayers talked about themselves (e.g., "I'd," "I'll," and "I'm"), defaulters tended to talk about others (e.g., "God," "he," or "mother"). In fact, when defaulters did include themselves in the conversation, they tended to talk about "we" rather than "I."

Intriguingly, many aspects of how defaulters wrote are associated with the writing style of liars and extroverts. While there was no evidence that defaulting borrowers were intentionally deceptive when writing their requests, intentionally or not, their writing may have reflected doubts about their ability to repay the loan.

Returning to the two people who asked for help fixing their roofs, both made persuasive pitches. Both seemed like nice people who would use the money for a good purpose.

Person 1	Person 2
I am a hardworking person, married for 25 years, and have two wonderful boys. Please let me explain why I need help. I would use the $2,000 loan to fix our roof. Thank you, God bless you, and I promise to pay you back.	While the past year in our new place has been more than great, the roof is now leaking, and I need to borrow $2,000 to cover the cost of the repair. I pay all bills (e.g., car loans, cable, utilities) on time.

But Person #2 is more likely to pay the money back. While Person #1 might have seemed more compelling, they're actually around 8 times more likely to default.*

People's words revealed their future actions. Even if they wanted to hide it, or didn't realize it themselves, what they were going to do leaked out through their language.

WHAT LANGUAGE TELLS US ABOUT SOCIETY

The fact that language reveals who wrote a play or whether someone will default on a bank loan is fascinating, but words can actually do a lot more. Because beyond telling us things about specific people, language also reveals things about society more broadly. The biases and beliefs that shape how we see the world.

Sexism is pervasive. From hiring and evaluation to recognition and compensation, women are often perceived less favorably and treated less fairly. Women are often paid less than men for the same job, for example, and the same résumé is seen as less qualified and offered a lower salary if it is associated with a female rather than male name.

But where do such biases come from? And how can they be mitigated?

When considering sexism, violent crime, or almost any other social

---

* Similar effects have been found in a host of domains. Online shoppers who use only lowercase when typing their name and shipping address, for example, are more than twice as likely not to pay for what they ordered. Shoppers whose email address includes their first and/or last name, however, are less likely to default.

ill, critics often blame culture. They argue that violent video games make people more violent or that misogynous music reinforces bias.

And there is some truth to this notion. Song lyrics that portray women negatively, for example, increase anti-female attitudes and misogynous behavior. Lyrics that espouse equality, however, can encourage pro-female behavior. Consequently, one reason that stereotypes and biases may be so persistent is that they are continually reinforced by the songs, books, movies, and other cultural items that we consume each day.

But while cultural items may have an impact, their actual makeup is less transparent. Consider music: Are song lyrics actually biased against women? And how have lyrics changed over time?

To answer this question Reihane Boghrati and I compiled more than a quarter of a million songs released from 1965 to 2018.[7] Everything from today's hits (by, e.g., John Mayer and Usher) and famous oldies (e.g., Gladys Knight's "Midnight Train to Georgia") to songs you never heard of, tens of thousands of songs from pop, rock, hip-hop, country, dance, and R&B.

And rather than have people listen to each song, which would be both time consuming and subjective, we used automated text analysis. Similar to the approach used by the Shakespeare detectives, we fed the lyrics of each song through an algorithm to understand whether songs talked about different genders differently. Not just whether the lyrics said explicitly positive or negative things, but whether they exhibited a more subtle, and potentially more impactful type of bias—like the one that often shows up when selecting job applicants.

Imagine that there are two job candidates, Mike and Susan. Both are stellar. Mike is really capable and experienced, and Susan is super-friendly and helpful. I can't sing either of their praises enough.

Noticed what happened there? Probably not. Because we tend to think about bias in a pretty explicit way.

If a recruiter treats men and women differently, they're clearly biased. Or if a résumé would be seen different if the candidate was named Dylan (a stereotypically White name) rather than DeAndre (a stereotypically African American name), it's easy to identify it as racism.

But it turns out that subtler forms of bias can be just as dangerous. Consider the way Mike and Susan were described. On the surface, both were talked about positively. But the *way* in which those words are positive differs.

Consistent with the words used to describe Mike ("capable" and "experienced"), men are often described based on their competence. How smart, intelligent, or successful they are, whether they are strategic thinkers, and how good they are at solving problems. Indeed, search for images of competent people and the results are almost twice as likely to feature men.[8]

When talking about women, however, people often focus on a different feature. Consistent with the words used to describe Susan ("friendly" and "caring"), women are often described based on their warmth. How nurturing, supportive, and agreeable they are, and whether they are good at building positive relationships or helping others develop. Search for images of warm people and almost two-thirds of the images will feature women.

The difference between warmth and competence may seem small, but it has big consequences. Hiring and promotion, for example, particularly for leadership roles, usually depend on how competent someone seems. And because the language used to describe women is less likely to focus on their competence, it puts women at a disadvantage.

We examined whether this linguistic difference might show up in music. Whether songs were less likely to focus on competence or intelligence when talking about women, for example, and whether this has changed over time.

The evidence was decidedly mixed. In some ways, things have improved. In the 1970s and early 1980s, lyrics were clearly biased against women. When songs talked about someone as being intelligent, clever, ambitious or brave, that person was much more likely to be a man than a woman. In the late '80s, and early '90s, though, things moved in a more equitable direction. Whether looking at pop music, dance, country, R&B, and even rock, things became more even, with women being talked about more similarly to men.

In the late 1990s, however, this progress reversed. Lyrics became more biased again and remain somewhat so to this day. Not as biased as they were in the 1970s, but certainly more so than the early 1990s.*

Further, these shifts seem to be driven by the language used by men. Female musicians' language didn't change much. Even going back to the 1970s they tended to talk about men and women similarly, and that persisted up to today. But male musicians' language showed a much greater shift: they started off biased in the 1970s, got better up until the early 1990s, and then the gains leveled off in the last few decades.

Music isn't the only domain that shows such gender differences. Children's books are dominated by male characters, and even when animals are used, they're three times more likely to be male.[9] In textbooks, three-quarters of the people mentioned are male,[10] in films, only 30 percent of speaking characters are women, in business school case studies, only 11 percent of protagonists are female.

----

* People often blame hip-hop for being particularly misogynous, and the genre rose in popularity in the early 1990s, so maybe that drove the shift. But blaming hip-hop is overly simplistic. Because a variety of other genres showed similar patterns. Country music, for example, also became more biased in the 1990s, as did R&B and dance to some degree.

And it's not just who gets mentioned. When they are mentioned, men and women get talked about differently.[11] When men and women are talked about in newspapers, men are more likely to have occupations like captain or boss, while women are more likely to have occupations like homemaker and receptionist. In movies, female characters talk less about things related to achievement. And in sports, female tennis players are twice as likely to be asked questions unrelated to tennis (e.g., where they got their nails done).

It's easy to blame individual people for this problem. After all, individual journalists picked individual people with different occupations and individual reporters asked individual tennis players different questions.

But aggregated together, these individual choices reveal a lot about the broader societies these individuals are a part of. Because if just a couple journalists or musicians were sexist, it would barely register. Those biased mentions would be swamped by the much larger percentage of people who were more equitable.

The fact that these biases persist across hundreds, thousands, or even millions of examples, however, suggests that something deeper is going on. Rather than reflecting something about a couple of individuals, and the individual choices they made, these linguistic breadcrumbs suggest the issues are much more acutely ingrained. That there are entrenched ways of seeing and treating different groups of people that may be much tougher to change.

And nowhere is this more visible than on issues of race.

RACISM AND POLICING

Breonna Taylor was killed on March 13, 2020. Soon after midnight, police officers burst into the twenty-six-year-old emergency room technician's apartment. Taylor was in bed at the time, and in the confusion that ensued, the police fired thirty-two times, striking Taylor six times and killing her.

George Floyd was murdered on May 25, 2020. Floyd had used a $20-dollar bill to buy a pack of cigarettes from a convenience store, and the clerk, thinking that the money was counterfeit, called the police. Seventeen minutes after the first police car arrived, Floyd was pinned beneath three officers, unconscious. Less than an hour later, he was pronounced dead.

These are only two examples of police force involving African Americans. The incidents sparked an outcry throughout the United States, led to a resurgence of the Black Lives Matter movement, and catalyzed national debates about race and policing.

Between those high-profile incidents, though, what is often lost is the everyday interactions between police officers and their communities.* By some estimates, more than 25 percent of the population comes into contact with a police officer at some point during a year, and the most common interaction is during a traffic stop.

Beyond their frequency, these interactions are quite consequential. Each one is an opportunity to build public trust in police or erode it, to strengthen the bridge with the community or undermine it.

But what are these everyday interactions like? And are Black and White community members treated differently?

The answer seems to depend on who you ask. Black community members report more negative experiences with police officers. They describe being treated less fairly, more harshly, and with less respect.

---

* Needless to say, these are complicated issues. Policemen and -women risk their lives every day to protect the communities they serve, and all citizens, regardless of race or ethnicity, have a right to safety, security, and equal treatment.

More than three-quarters of African Americans, for example, said police do not treat Blacks as fairly as they do Whites.[12]

Police officers, not surprisingly, see things differently. Most reject the notion that their behavior is biased.[13] They see the deaths of Black people as isolated incidents that are driven by a few bad apples or the circumstances at hand. Many believe that officers are simply targeting criminal behavior and that rather than being driven by bias, any differences in treatment are driven by racial differences in who is committing crimes.

So which is it?

In 2017, scientists from Stanford University tried to find out.[14] Police-community interactions obviously depend on a host of complicated factors, but to begin to understand what might be going on, the researchers focused on language. How officers talk to White and Black community members.

Working with the city of Oakland, California, the scientists examined body camera footage from thousands of routine traffic stops. They analyzed hundreds of cases where Black motorists were stopped and a similar number where the motorist was White.

Such interactions often follow a common script. A motorist is stopped for driving too fast or having an expired registration. After taking some notes, checking the license plate, and making sure that everything else is in order, the officer often walks up to the driver's-side window.

When things go well, a conversation ensues. The officer explains why the motorist was stopped and asks for license and registration to run some background checks. The motorist provides the information and waits patiently while any necessary checks are run. Eventually the situation is resolved and the two parties part ways. The motorist may receive a ticket or instruction to get something fixed, but everything ends amicably.

Not all conversations, though, are this straightforward, and there are many ways the interaction can go sideways. The officer may be concerned that the motorist is armed, drunk, or on drugs. The motorist may feel scared or anxious and lash out verbally or otherwise. Things can quickly get out of hand.

While both sides obviously play a role, the words officers use are critical. They can communicate respect and understanding or contempt and disregard. They can calm a worried motorist down or make them more anxious.

By parsing the language officers used, the researchers tested whether White and Black drivers were treated with differing degrees of respect. Watching every single stop would be time consuming, and the researchers' own biases could affect their judgments, so they let the language speak for itself. They used machine learning to objectively measure and quantify the language used.

The findings were striking. Hundreds of hours of interactions showed that the language used toward Black drivers was less polite, less friendly, and less respectful.

When talking to White motorists, for example, officers were more likely to use formal titles (e.g., "sir" or "ma'am"), offer reassurance (e.g., "It's okay," "Don't worry," or "No problem"), or offer the motorist agency (e.g., "You can ____" or "You could____"). They were more likely to use the motorist's last name, talk about safety, or use positive words.

When talking to Black motorists, however, officers were more likely to use informal titles (e.g., "Dude," "Bud," or "Champ"), ask questions, or tell them to keep their hands on the wheel. Put simply, the findings demonstrate that "police interactions with black community members are more fraught than their interactions with white community members."

To be fair, one could wonder whether these differences are driven by something other than race. Maybe officers are more polite to White motorists because the White motorists who were stopped happened to be older or were more likely to be female. Alternatively, maybe the differences were due to the severity of the offense. If some motorists were stopped for more minor things (e.g., a broken taillight) and others were stopped for more major ones, maybe the offense itself drove the linguistic differences. Or maybe the differences were due to the race of the officer who was speaking or whether a search was being conducted.

Even controlling for all those aspects, though, the results still held. Officers spoke to Black community members with less respect. Even considering someone who was the same age and gender and stopped in the same part of town for the same type of issue, officers' language was more respectful when the person was White.

And the difference wasn't driven by just a couple of rogue officers. Among hundreds of officers, whether White, Black, Hispanic, Asian, or other, the pattern persisted: Black motorists were treated with less respect.

As one researcher noted, "If we just look at the words that were used by the officer, we can predict the race of the person that they were talking to about two-thirds of the time."

While White motorists are more likely to hear something like "There you go, ma'am. Drive safe please" or "No problem. Thank you very much, sir," Black motorists tended to hear something quite different. Phrases like "Can I see that driver's license again?" or "All right, my man. Do me a favor. Just keep your hands on the steering wheel real quick."*

Taken together, these seemingly small differences added up to pervasive racial disparities.

The Stanford study raises a host of important questions. It's easy to call police officers racist or point to this as evidence that the police are out to get African Americans. And that is certainly one way to see the results.

But the truth is likely both subtler and more complex.

Some individual officers may be racist. And given the broader actions of individual officers in particular high-profile cases, this is almost certainly the case.

But regardless, even if it isn't intentional, a much larger portion of officers are treating White and Black people differently. Most officers likely mean well and are simply doing the best they can in difficult situations. But whether they realize it or not and whether they mean to or not, the words they use differ. And this makes the underlying problem even more challenging to solve.

Because it's one thing to identify a few bad officers. To root out the bad apples and get rid of them.

But changing ingrained stereotypes, associations, habits, and

---

* Race even impacted subtle things like tone. When talking to Black motorists, officers sounded more negative. They seemed more tense, less friendly, and less respectful. They were also more likely to talk down to Blacks than to Whites. Not surprisingly, these linguistic differences had important consequences. Compared to the tone used with White motorists, hearing the tone officers used with Black motorists reduced trust in the police department and suggested that officers cared less about their community.

responses of hundreds of thousands of officers requires much more effort.*

The good news, though, is that language can help. Because even if almost all officers mean well, and are trying to do the right thing, their language helps identify areas for improvement. Places where even if they didn't realize it, they are treating people differently. And by identifying even unintentional bias, hopefully things can be nudged in the right direction.

---

* Not that bias isn't just about police officers or traffic stops. Books are biased against Asian Americans (i.e., more likely to call them passive or effeminate), news articles are biased against Islam (i.e., more likely to connect it to terrorism), and there are numerous other ways that culture is often biased. By realizing these subtle biases, hopefully we can begin to address them.

Epilogue

Throughout the book, we've talked about the power of magic words. How the words we use, and the way we use them, can have a big impact on our happiness and success. Helping us persuade others, deepen social bonds, and communicate more effectively.

First, we talked about the language of *identity* and *agency*. How rather than just conveying requests or information, words can indicate who's in charge, who's to blame, and what it means to engage in a particular action. We learned how to increase our influence by turning actions into identity (i.e., help ➡ helper or vote ➡ voter), stick to our goals by changing *can't*s into *don't*s, and be a more creative problem solver by turning *could*s into *should*s. We explored why talking to ourselves can be a helpful tool to reduce anxiety and improve performance and when words like "you" are helpful versus detrimental.

Second, we discussed the language of *confidence*. How beyond communicating facts and opinions, words communicate how certain we are about those facts and opinions. We discovered why the way lawyers talk can be just as important as the facts they share, how to speak with power, and why we should turn pasts into presents (i.e., why saying a restaurant "has" rather than "had" great food will make other people more likely to go there). Along the way we learned the words that make communicators seem more credible, trustworthy, and authoritative, and when it's better to seem certain versus express doubt. When to ditch hedges (e.g., "may" or "I think") and hesitations (e.g., "um" or "er") and when they might not be as detrimental.

Third, we explored the language of *questions*. While we often think of questions as simply helping us collect information, they do a lot more. We learned why asking for advice can actually help make us seem more competent and why speed daters who ask more questions are more likely to get a second date. But beyond the benefits of questions in general, we also learned which types of questions are most effective and the right time to ask them; why follow-up questions are particularly beneficial; how to use questions to deflect and how to ask questions that avoid assumptions; and how to deepen social bonds with anyone, from strangers to colleagues, by asking the right questions in the right order (i.e., start safe, then build).

Fourth, we talked about the language of *concreteness*. Whether we're talking to customers, colleagues, family, or friends, we often fall prey to the curse of knowledge. We communicate in a high-level way that we think is easy to understand but goes right over the heads of our listeners. Linguistic concreteness can help. We discussed how to show listening, why talking about "fixing" rather than "solving" problems improves customer satisfaction, and why talking about a "gray T-shirt" rather than a "top" increases sales. We explored why specific, vivid language helps show we're listening, encourages attention, and makes ideas easier to understand. But we also reviewed when it's better to be abstract. Why using abstract language can help startups raise funding or signal leadership potential.

Fifth, we discussed the language of *emotion*. Sometimes people think facts sell ideas, but that belief is often misguided. Emotional language can be a powerful way to grab attention, captivate an audience, and persuade people to take action. We explored what makes a good story and the value of low points to make high points more impactful. But we also talked about why it's important to consider the context and think beyond just positivity and negativity. Why "amazing" and "perfect" are both positive words, but why which one to use depends on the type of context we're in (i.e., more hedonic or more utilitarian). And how to craft presentations, stories, and content that will engage interest, regardless of the topic.

Sixth, we explored the language of *similarity* (and difference): how people who write more similarly to their colleagues are more likely to get promoted and couples who talk more similarly are more likely to go on a second date. But lest it seem as though signaling similarity is always good, we talked about when and why difference is better; why popular songs tend to be different from their genres and unusually worded quotes are easier to remember; how language can help quantify the speed of stories, when it's better to move faster versus slower, and how the volume and circuitousness of movies, TV shows, and books predict whether they will succeed or fail.

Though distinct, these six types of magic words can help us across all areas of our lives.

Further, while the first six chapters focused on language's impact, or how words and phrases can be used to influence others, the last chapter examined a different way words are magical: what they reveal about the people and society that created them. How researchers identified Shakespeare's long-lost play without even reading it and why the words potential borrowers use in a loan application shed light on how likely they are to default. How analyzing hundreds of thousands of songs answered the age-old question of whether music is misogynous (and whether it's changed over time) and what police language can tell us about subtle racial bias.

Magic words are often used to describe language that has an amazing impact. By uttering phrases like "Abracadabra!," "Hocus-pocus," or "Open sesame!," magicians and mystics were able to do things that seemed impossible.

Indeed, as we've shown throughout the book, the right words used at the right time can have immense power. They can help us persuade colleagues and customers, engage audiences and acquaintances, and connect with partners and peers.

But while the impact of these words may seem magical, we don't have to be a magician to use them. Indeed, rather than being a spell, or some black box of undetermined origin, these words work by leveraging the science of human behavior.

By understanding how magic words work, anyone can harness their power.

The book started with a story about Jasper, and his discovery of the magic word "please." And as he gets older, it's fun to see how he discovers words and what they mean. He's a sponge. One day, out of the blue, he started saying the word "basically," probably because he heard someone else use it. Another day he started saying he needed something *immediately*, likely for similar reasons.

He's also started critiquing how I use words. One day, I told him that I *needed* him to put his jacket on. He replied that I didn't *need* him to put his jacket on, I just *wanted* him to. We'll see what he comes up with next.

There's one piece of research, though, that I think about a lot.

Parenting often feels a little bit like being a sheep dog. Your job is to encourage someone to move in the right direction, but most of the time they're more interested in doing something else. So you have to nudge, coax, and cajole them. Ask them to put their shoes on. Remind them not to push their sister. Ask them again to put their shoes on, this time with a slightly stronger tone.

Praise seems a lot easier. When kids figure something out by themselves, show off something they've drawn, or bring home an A on a math test, it's a chance to celebrate and applaud what they've done.

In the late 1990s, though, two behavioral scientists from Columbia University wondered whether *how* we praise might matter.[1] Specifically, whether using certain words when doling out approval might shape people's motivation.

They took a bunch of fifth graders and asked them to solve some abstract reasoning problems. Things like looking at a series of shapes and figuring out which of several options went next in the series.

The students worked on the problems for a few minutes, and then the researchers gave them feedback on how they were doing. All the students were told they had done well ("Wow, you did very well on these problems") but in addition, some students also were praised for their ability, in this case, intelligence ("You must be smart at these problems").

The researchers picked that form of praise because it is a standard approach for a job well done. When students get the right answer or employees solve a tough problem, we often praise them for their intelligence. We commend them for being smart or clever, thinking that will encourage them to keep learning, working hard, or putting in effort. But the researchers wondered what would happen when praise recipients encountered adversity. When things got tougher or they floundered a bit.

So after receiving the initial positive feedback, the students were given more difficult problems to solve. This time, they were told they had done poorly ("a lot worse") and solved less than half the problems they tried. Everyone then received a third set of problems, of similar difficulty to the first ones, and the researchers observed how well they did.

The students who hadn't been praised did about as well as they had done before, no better and no worse. They solved a similar number of problems and had a fine time doing it.

But the students who had been praised for their ability, in particular their intelligence, did more poorly. Rather than helping their performance, praise of their ability decreased it. The students who had been praised for their intelligence solved fewer problems than they had previously and did even worse than the students who hadn't been praised at all.

And there were a host of other negative consequences as well: not only did praising students for their intelligence make them perform worse, they ended up liking solving puzzles less and became less interested in persisting in solving them.

Praising their ability changed how students saw things. Rather than being interested in learning or enjoying solving the puzzles, it led them to see puzzle solving as a chance to show how smart they were. Intelligence became a fixed thing they either had or didn't have. And if success meant that they were smart, failure meant that they were stupid—which made them less interested in trying hard when they encountered setbacks.

But that doesn't mean all praise is detrimental.

For another set of students, the researchers worded the praise slightly differently. Rather than praising the *person*, or telling them how smart they were, the researchers praised the *process*, or how hard they were working ("You must have worked hard at these problems").

As with many ideas we've talked about throughout the book, the difference between these approaches may seem strikingly small. After all, all the students were told that they had done well, and only two or three words were changed in what was said.

But those two or three words made a big difference. Rather than hurting their motivation, praising the students' process, or how hard they had worked, encouraged them to keep going. They were more motivated, solved more puzzles, and enjoyed the experience more. They were more interested in learning and less interested in just doing well, and that shift in mindset led them to do better as a result.

Telling someone they're smart, good at math, or a great presenter implies that their performance depends on a stable trait. If they did well on a test, they have that trait, but if they did badly, well, they're just out of luck. They don't have what it takes and there's not much they can do to change it.

But rephrasing that feedback as process praise is more likely to have the intended effect. Telling someone they *did* well, or *did* a good job *on* a test or presentation, focuses less on stable traits and more on the particular instance at hand.* Which means if things don't go so well once in a while, it's not a mark of failure or lack of ability. It's just a misstep and reminder to work harder next time around.

A few (magic) words can make all the difference.

----

* It's the same with things such as "Great job, you must have worked really hard!" or "You really studied, and your improvement shows it."

Appendix

Reference Guide for Using and Applying Natural Language Processing

For the most part, this book has focused on individuals and how by understanding the new science of language, we can increase our influence and be more successful, in both our personal and professional lives.

But the same tools outlined here are equally useful for companies and organizations. Here are just a couple of examples of how they are being deployed.

CUSTOMER ANALYTICS

One place many companies are using natural language processing is in customer analytics. Using what customers, or potential customers, write or say to help predict their future behavior or encourage desired actions.

Take segmentation, for example. Some number of customers may have issues or complaints, but how do we know which ones to route where? By using their words, we can get a better sense of what they are looking for and whom to connect them to. We can even use machine learning to figure out who might be more likely to cancel their service, and try to intervene.

The same ideas can be applied to potential customers. Social media data provides a wealth of information about who someone is and what they care about. Companies use such information to target their ads, figuring out who to show which message based on the likelihood of conversion. Look-alike targeting, for example, finds people who are as similar as possible to existing customers on observable attributes and uses that to determine which potential customers might be most interested in a product or service.

Companies can also use language to learn about products to launch or problems to address. An approach called "social listening" combs social media data to understand how people are talking about a product, service, or idea. A hotel might learn that many consumers are complaining about the beds, for example, and use that to make a change. A drug maker might learn about emerging side effects or customer concerns.

Alternatively, the same data can be used in new-product development. By understanding what consumers are unhappy with about existing products and services, companies can determine how to best roll out new ones. Similarly, internet search data can be used to understand where opportunities are in a market or where interest is high.

LEGAL CASES

Language can also be used in interesting ways in legal cases. Say a detergent brand is being accused of greenwashing. The allegations suggest that the brand has been falsely marketing themselves as eco-friendly when they're really not. The standard approach might be to ask experts to opine on what they think is going on. An expert for the plaintiff could highlight a particular advertisement, for example, and argue that because it shows a picture of trees, or the earth, it must mean that the brand is marketing itself as eco-friendly.

But while this is a fine opinion, and may even be correct, the problem is it's just that. An opinion. It's pretty subjective.

A defense expert could look at the exact same advertisement and generate a completely different opinion based on the side they're supporting. The ad also talks about cleaning effectiveness, for example, so they could use that as indication that the brand isn't actually arguing they're eco-friendly.

So which is it?

Rather than one expert making a guesstimate, and the other side doing something similar, text analysis can provide a more realistic picture of what happened. By aggregating language from a large number of advertisements (or social media posts made by the brand), we can get a more accurate sense of what is going on.

A simple place to start would just count individual words. Take a list of environmental words (e.g., earth, environment, and eco-friendly), and count the number of times they appear. What percentage of ads, or social media posts, use at least one of these words? Further, is this language prevalent over time, or just a few ads that show up in a particular geography?

More complex techniques can shed even more light. By comparing the language used by the detergent brand, and comparing it to the language used by other brands either known to be eco-friendly (e.g., Seventh Generation or Tide purclean) or not (e.g., Gain or regular Tide), one can get a more objective answer.

Using data from thousands of ads or posts by dozens of other brands known to pitch themselves as eco-friendly or not, one can train a machine-learning classifier to identify the degree to which a particular ad or post is pitching a brand as eco-friendly. Then, by running all the at-issue brand's ads and posts through the classifier, we can get a sense of whether, on average, the detergent brand is actually marketing themselves as eco-friendly.

One could use similar techniques to measure whether an alcohol brand's advertising is youth targeting, or a politician is talking more like a Democrat or a Republican.

Automated text analysis is particularly useful in these and similar examples because it allows us to travel back in time.

Say a technology company is being accused of false advertising. It claimed that its laptop was as "light as a feather" in a couple of its ads, and a lawsuit alleges that consumers bought the laptop based on that false claim.

One standard approach would be to use surveys. Take a set of consumers, show them the ad, and see whether they are more interested in buying the laptop than consumers who didn't see the ad.

Unfortunately, that still doesn't resolve the issue, because although the survey results suggest what consumers' reaction is to seeing the ad *today*, it says less about what their reaction was, or would have been, if they had seen the ad when it ran a couple years ago. Context changes; a particular claim may have had one effect two years ago but have a completely different effect today.

Consequently, unless we can invent a time machine, it's almost impossible to know how people felt two years ago.

But text analysis can do just that.

By analyzing social media posts or product reviews, we can get a better sense of whether people picked up on that claim and whether it shaped their attitude toward the laptop. By examining posts consumers wrote about the product before and after the ads ran, for example, we can get a sense of whether they changed how positively they felt about it. Similarly, by delving deeper into the content of those posts, we can see not only whether consumers said more positive things but whether they actually mentioned attributes such as the laptop's weight when doing so.

Mass media language can also be useful. By analyzing the words used in newspaper articles about the product, we can see whether or not the media actually picked up on the claims made by the brand.

Time travel is still impossible, but text analysis enables a new type of archaeology. Like fossils from an ancient civilization or an insect preserved in amber, decades-old thoughts, opinions, and attitudes are hidden in digitized language. And automated text analysis provides the tools to unlock the insights hidden within.

SOME EASILY ACCESSIBLE TOOLS

This book has focused on the insights gained from language, but some people may be interested in applying some of the tools mentioned. Here are two that are easy to play around with.

- https://liwc.app/: A great resource for scoring texts on a variety of psychological dimensions
- http://textanalyzer.org/: A useful tool for scoring other dimenions and extracting basic topics or themes

If you're interested in more complex tools or how they can be used in a variety of settings, here are two recent review papers that discuss various methodologies:

- Jonah Berger and Grant Packard, "Using natural language processing to understand people and culture." *American Psychologist*, 77(4), 525–537.
- Jonah Berger, Ashlee Humphreys, Stephen Ludwig, Wendy Moe, Oded Netzer, and David Schweidel, "Uniting the Tribes: Using Text for Marketing Insight," *Journal of Marketing* 84, no. 1 (2020): 1–25.

Acknowledgments

This book would not have been possible without Grant Packard, a collaborator, colleague, and friend who taught me basically everything I know about language. I hope we have many more years of successful collaborations. Thanks to Hollis Heimbouch and James Neidhardt for useful feedback along the way, to Jim Levine for ever-consistent guidance and support, and to Noah Katz for help with figures and references. Thanks to Maria and Jamie, for introducing me to a world of new language puzzles, to Jamie Pennebaker for all his amazing work in this space, and to Lilly and Caroline, for loving books. Finally, thanks to Jordan, Jasper, Jesse, and Zoe for making every day magical.

Notes

Introduction

1. Matthias R. Mehl et al., "Are Women Really More Talkative than Men?," *Science* 317, no. 5834 (2007): 82, doi.org/10.1126/science.1139940.
2. Ellen J. Langer, Arthur Blank, and Benzion Chanowitz, "The Mindlessness of Ostensibly Thoughtful Action: The Role of 'Placebic' Information in Interpersonal Interaction," *Journal of Personality and Social Psychology* 36, no. 6 (1978): 635.

Chapter 1: Activate Identity and Agency

1. Christopher J. Bryan, Allison Master, and Gregory M. Walton, "'Helping' Versus 'Being a Helper': Invoking the Self to Increase Helping in Young Children," *Child Development* 85, no. 5 (2014): 1836–42, https://doi.org/10.1111/cdev.12244.
2. Susan A. Gelman and Gail D. Heyman, "Carrot-Eaters and Creature-Believers: The Effects of Lexicalization on Children's Inferences About Social Categories," *Psychological Science* 10, no. 6 (1999): 489–93, https://doi.org/10.1111/1467-9280.00194.
3. Gregory M. Walton and Mahzarin R. Banaji, "Being What You Say: The Effect of Essentialist Linguistic Labels on Preferences," *Social Cognition* 22, no. 2 (2004): 193–213, https://doi.org/10.1521/soco.22.2.193.35463.
4. Christopher J. Bryan et al., "Motivating Voter Turnout by Invoking the Self," *Proceedings*

of the National Academy of Sciences of the United States of America 108, no. 31 (2011): 12653–56, https://doi.org/10.1073/pnas.1103343108.

5. Christopher J. Bryan, Gabrielle S. Adams, and Benoit Monin, "When Cheating Would Make You a Cheater: Implicating the Self Prevents Unethical Behavior," *Journal of Experimental Psychology: General* 142, no. 4 (2013): 1001, https://doi.org/10.1037/a0030655.

6. Vanessa M. Patrick, and Henrik Hagtvedt, "'I don't' Versus 'I can't': When Empowered Refusal Motivates Goal-Directed Behavior," *Journal of Consumer Research* 39, no. 2 (2012): 371–81, https://doi.org/10.1086/663212. Also see Vanessa Patrick's amazing book *The Power of Saying No: The New Science of How to Say No that Puts You in Charge of Your Life*. Sourcebooks.

7. Ting Zhang, Francesca Gino, and Joshua D. Margolis, "Does 'Could' Lead to Good? On the Road to Moral Insight," *Academy of Management Journal* 61, no. 3 (2018): 857–95, https://doi.org/10.5465/amj.2014.0839.

8. Ellen J. Langer and Alison I. Piper, "The Prevention of Mindlessness," *Journal of Personality and Social Psychology* 53, no. 2 (1857): 280, https://doi.org/10.1037/0022-3514.53.2.280.

9. Ethan Kross has done some great work in this space; see his book *Chatter: The Voice in Our Head, Why it Matters, and How to Harness It* (New York: Crown, 2021).

10. Ethan Kross et al., "Third-Person Self-Talk Reduces Ebola Worry and Risk Perception by Enhancing Rational Thinking," *Applied Psychology: Health and Well-Being* 9, no. 3 (2017): 387–409, https://doi.org/10.1111/aphw.12103; Celina R. Furman, Ethan Kross, and Ashley N. Gearhardt, "Distanced Self-Talk Enhances Goal Pursuit to Eat Healthier," *Clinical Psychological Science* 8, no. 2 (2020): 366–73, https://doi.org/10.1177/2167702619896366.

11. Antonis Hatzigeorgiadis et al., "Self-Talk and Sports Performance: A Meta-analysis," *Perspectives on Psychological Science* 6, no. 4 (2011): 348–56, https://doi.org/10.1177/1745691611413136.

12. Ryan E. Cruz, James M. Leonhardt, and Todd Pezzuti, "Second Person Pronouns Enhance Consumer Involvement and Brand Attitude," *Journal of Interactive Marketing* 39 (2017): 104–16, https://10.1016/j.intmar.2017.05.001.

13. Grant Packard, Sarah G. Moore, and Brent McFerran, "(I'm) Happy to Help (You): The Impact of Personal Pronoun Use in Customer-Firm Interactions," *Journal of Marketing Research* 55, no. 5 (2018): 541–55, https://doi.org/10.1509/jmr.16.0118.

Chapter 2: Convey Confidence

1. William M. O'Barr, *Linguistic Evidence: Language, Power, and Strategy in the Courtroom* (New York: Academic Press, 2014).

2. Bonnie E. Erickson et al., "Speech Style and Impression Formation in a Court Setting: The Effects of 'Powerful' and 'Powerless' Speech," *Journal of Experimental Social Psychology* 14, no. 3 (1978): 266–79, https://doi.org/10.1016/0022-1031(78)90015-X.

3. Some examples of this work include: Mark Adkins and Dale E. Brashers, "The Power of Language in Computer-Mediated Groups," *Management Communication Quarterly* 8, no. 3 (1995): 289–322, https://doi.org/10.1177/0893318995008003002; Lawrence

A. Hosman, "The Evaluative Consequences of Hedges, Hesitations, and Intensifies: Powerful and Powerless Speech Styles," *Human Communication Research* 15, no. 3 (1989): 383–406, https://doi.org/10.1111/j.1468-2958.1989.tb00190.x; Nancy A. Burell and Randal J. Koper, "The Efficacy of Powerful/Powerless Language on Attitudes and Source Credibility," in *Persuasion: Advances Through Meta-analysis*, edited by Michael Allen and Raymond W Preiss (Creskill, NJ: Hamapton Press, 1988): 203–15; Charles S. Areni and John R. Sparks, "Language Power and Persuasion," *Psychology & Marketing* 22, no. 6 (2005): 507–25, https://doi.org/10.1002/mar.20071; John R. Sparks, Charles S. Areni, and K. Chris Cox, "An Investigation of the Effects of Language Style and Communication Modality on Persuasion," *Communications Monographs* 65, no. 2 (1998): 108–25, https://doi.org/10.1080/03637759809376440.

4. Paul C. Price and Eric R. Stone, "Intuitive Evaluation of Likelihood Judgment Producers: Evidence for a Confidence Heuristic," *Journal of Behavioral Decision Making* 17, no. 1 (2004): 39–57, https://doi.org/10.1002/bdm.460.

5. Indeed, researchers whose grant proposals use less tentative language and more certain language get more funding from the National Science Foundation. See David M. Markowitz, "What Words Are Worth: National Science Foundation Grant Abstracts Indicate Award Funding," *Journal of Language and Social Psychology* 38, no. 3 (2019): 264–82, https://doi.org/10.1177/0261927X18824859.

6. Lawrence A. Hosman, "The Evaluative Consequences of Hedges, Hesitations, and Intensifiers: Powerful and Powerless Speech Styles," *Human Communication Research* 15, no. 3 (1989): 383–406; James J. Bradac and Anthony Mulac, "A Molecular View of Powerful and Powerless Speech Styles: Attributional Consequences of Specific Language Features and Communicator Intentions," *Communications Monographs* 51, no. 4 (1984): 307–19, https://doi.org/10.1080/03637758409390204.

7. Laurie L. Haleta, "Student Perceptions of Teachers' Use of Language: The Effects of Powerful and Powerless Language on Impression Formation and Uncertainty," *Communication Education* 45, no. 1 (1996): 16–28, https://doi.org/10.1080/0363452960937 9029.

8. David Hagmann and George Loewenstein, "Persuasion with Motivated Beliefs," in *Opinion Dynamics & Collective Decisions Workshop* (2017).

9. Mohamed A. Hussein and Zakary L. Tormala, "Undermining Your Case to Enhance Your Impact: A Framework for Understanding the Effects of Acts of Receptiveness in Persuasion," *Personality and Social Psychology Review* 25, no. 3 (2021): 229–50, https://doi.org/10.1177/10888683211001269.

10. Jakob D. Jensen, "Scientific Uncertainty in News Coverage of Cancer Research: Effects of Hedging on Scientists' and Journalists' Credibility," *Human Communication Research* 34, no. 3 (2008): 347–69, https://doi.org/10.1111/j.1468-2958.2008.00324.x.

Chapter 3: Ask the Right Questions

1. Alison Wood Brooks, Francesca Gino, and Maurice E. Schweitzer, "Smart People Ask for (My) Advice: Seeking Advice Boosts Perceptions of Competence," *Management Science* 61, no. 6 (2015): 1421–35, https://doi.org/10.1287/mnsc.2014.2054.

2. Daniel A. McFarland, Dan Jurafsky, and Craig Rawlings, "Making the Connection:

Social Bonding in Courtship Situations," *American Journal of Sociology* 118, no. 6 (2013): 1596–1649.

3. Karen Huang et al., "It Doesn't Hurt to Ask: Question-Asking Increases Liking," *Journal of Personality and Social Psychology* 113, no. 3 (2017): 430, https://doi.org/10.1037/pspi0000097.

4. Klea D. Bertakis, Debra Roter, and Samuel M. Putnam, "The Relationship of Physician Medical Interview Style to Patient Satisfaction," *Journal of Family Practice* 32, no. 2 (1991): 175–81.

5. Bradford T. Bitterly and Maurice E. Schweitzer, "The Economic and Interpersonal Consequences of Deflecting Direct Questions," *Journal of Personality and Social Psychology* 118, no. 5 (2020): 945, https://doi.org/10.1037/pspi0000200.

6. Julia A. Minson et al., "Eliciting the Truth, the Whole Truth, and Nothing but the Truth: The Effect of Question Phrasing on Deception," *Organizational Behavior and Human Decision Processes* 147 (2018): 76–93, https://doi.org/10.1016/j.obhdp.2018.05.006.

7. Arthur Aron et al., "The Experimental Generation of Interpersonal Closeness: A Procedure and Some Preliminary Findings," *Personality and Social Psychology Bulletin* 23, no. 4 (1997): 363–77.

8. Elizabeth Page-Gould, Rodolfo Mendoza-Denton, and Linda R. Tropp, "With a Little Help from My Cross-Group Friend: Reducing Anxiety in Intergroup Contexts Through Cross-Group Friendship," *Journal of Personality and Social Psychology* 95, no. 5 (2008): 1080, https://doi.org/10.1037/0022-3514.95.5.1080.

Chapter 4: Leverage Concreteness

1. Grant Packard and Jonah Berger, "How Concrete Language Shapes Customer Satisfaction," *Journal of Consumer Research* 47, no. 5 (2021): 787–806, https://10.1093/jcr/ucaa038.

2. Nooshin L. Warren et al., "Marketing Ideas: How to Write Research Articles That Readers Understand and Cite," *Journal of Marketing* 85, no. 5 (2021): 42–57, https://doi.org/10.1177/00222429211003560.

3. Ian Begg, "Recall of Meaningful Phrases," *Journal of Verbal Learning and Verbal Behavior* 11, no. 4 (1972): 431–39, https://doi.org/10.1016/S0022-5371(72)80024-0.

4. Jonah Berger, Wendy Moe, and David Schweidel, "Linguistic Drivers of Content Consumption," working paper, 2022; Yoon Koh et al., "Successful Restaurant Crowdfunding: The Role of Linguistic Style," *International Journal of Contemporary Hospitality Management* 32, no. 10 (2020): 3051–66, https://doi.org/10.1108/IJCHM-02-2020-0159.

5. Colin Camerer, George Loewenstein, and Martin Weber, "The Curse of Knowledge in Economic Settings: An Experimental Analysis," *Journal of Political Economy* 97, no. 5 (1989): 1232–54. See also Chip Heath and Dan Heath, *Made to Stick: Why Some Ideas Survive and Others Die* (New York: Random House, 2007).

6. Laura Huang et al., "Sizing Up Entrepreneurial Potential: Gender Differences in Communication and Investor Perceptions of Long-Term Growth and Scalability," *Academy of Management Journal* 64, no. 3 (2021): 716–40, https://doi.org/10.5465/amj.2018.1417.

7. Cheryl J. Wakslak, Pamela K. Smith, and Albert Han, "Using Abstract Language Signals

Power," *Journal of Personality and Social Psychology* 107, no. 1 (2014): 41, https://doi
.org/10.1037/a0036626.

Chapter 5: Employ Emotion

1. Elliot Aronson et al., "The Effect of a Pratfall on Increasing Interpersonal Attractive-
    ness," *Psychonomic Science* 4, no. 6 (1966): 227–28, https://doi.org/10.3758/BF033
    42263.
2. See also Andrew J. Reagan et al., "The Emotional Arcs of Stories Dominated by Six
    Basic Shapes," *EPJ Data Science* 5, no. 1 (2016): 1–12, https://doi.org/10.1140/epjds
    /s13688-016-0093-1.
3. Peter Sheridan Dodds et al., "Temporal Patterns of Happiness and Information in a
    Global Social Network: Hedonometrics and Twitter," *PLOS ONE*, December 7, 2011,
    https://doi.org/10.1371/journal.pone.0026752.
4. Erik Lindqvist, Robert Ostling, and David Cesarini, "Long-Run Effects of Lottery
    Wealth on Psychological Well-Being," *Review of Economic Studies* 87, no. 6 (2020):
    2703–26, https://doi.org/10.1093/restud/rdaa006.
5. Shane Fredrick and George Loewenstein, in *Well-Being: The Foundations of Hedonic
    Psychology*, edited by D. Kahneman, E. Diener, and N. Schwarz (New York: Russell
    Sage, 1999), 302–29.
6. Leif D. Nelson, Tom Meyvis, and Jeff Galak, "Enhancing the Television-Viewing Ex-
    perience Through Commercial Interruption," *Journal of Consumer Research* 36, no. 2
    (2009): 160–72, https://doi.org/10.1086/597030.
7. Bart De Langhe, Philip M. Fernbach, and Donald R. Lichtenstein, "Navigating by
    the Stars: Investigating the Actual and Perceived Validity of Online User Ratings,"
    Journal of Consumer Research 42, no. 6 (2016): 817–33, https://doi.org/10.1093/jcr
    /ucv047.
8. Matthew D. Rocklage, Derek D. Rucker, and Loran F. Nordgren, "Mass-Scale Emo-
    tionality Reveals Human Behaviour and Marketplace Success," *Nature Human Behav-
    ior* 5 (2021): 1323–29, https://doi.org/10.1038/s41562-021-01098-5.
9. For more examples of words that vary on these different dimensions, see The Evalua-
    tive Lexicon (http://www.evaluativelexicon.com/) and Matthew D. Rocklage, Derek
    D. Rucker, and Loren F. Nordgren, "The Evaluative Lexicon 2.0: The Measurement of
    Emotionality, Extremity, and Valence in Language," *Behavior Research Methods* 50,
    no. 4 (2018): 1327–44, https://doi.org/10.3758/s13428-017-0975-6.
10. Rocklage et al., "Mass-Scale Emotionality Reveals Human Behaviour and Market-
    place Success."
11. Jonah Berger, Matthew D. Rocklage, and Grant Packard , "Expression Modalities: How
    Speaking Versus Writing Shapes Word of Mouth," *Journal of Consumer Research*,
    December 25, 2021, https://doi.org/10.1093/jcr/ucab076.
12. Matthew D. Rocklage and Russell H. Fazio, "The Enhancing Versus Backfiring Effects
    of Positive Emotion in Consumer Reviews," *Journal of Marketing Research* 57, no. 2
    (2020): 332–52, https://doi.org/10.1177/0022243719892594.
13. Li, Yang, Grant Packard, and Jonah Berger, "When Employee Language Matters?"
    Working Paper.

Chapter 6: Harness Similarity (and Difference)

1. Amir Goldberg et al., "Enculturation Trajectories and Individual Attainment: An Interactional Language Use Model of Cultural Dynamics in Organizations," in Wharton People Analytics Conference, Philadelphia, PA, 2016.

2. James W. Pennebaker et al., "When Small Words Foretell Academic Success: The Case of College Admissions Essays," *PLOS ONE*, December 31, 2014: e115844, https://doi.org/10.1371/journal.pone.0115844.

3. See, e.g., Molly E. Ireland et al., "Language Style Matching Predicts Relationship Initiation and Stability," *Psychological Science* 22, no. 1 (2011): 39–44, https://doi.org/10.1177/0956797610392928; Balazs Kovacs and Adam M. Kleinbaum, "Language-Style Similarity and Social Networks," *Psychological Science* 31, no. 2 (2020): 202–13, https://doi.org/10.1177/0956797619894557.

4. Jonah Berger and Grant Packard, "Are Atypical Things More Popular?," *Psychological Science* 29, no. 7 (2018): 1178–84, https://doi.org/10.1177/0956797618759465.

5. David M. Blei, Andrew Y. Ng, and Michael I. Jordan, "Latent Dirichlet Allocation," *Journal of Machine Learning Research* 3 (2003): 993–1022, https://www.jmlr.org/papers/volume3/blei03a/blei03a.pdf.

6. Ireland et al., "Language Style Matching Predicts Relationship Initiation and Stability"; Paul J. Taylor and Sally Thomas, "Linguistic Style Matching and Negotiation Outcome," *Negotiation and Conflict Management Research* 1, no. 3 (2008): 263–81, https://doi.org/10.1111/j.1750-4716.2008.00016.x.

7. Kurt Gray et al., "'Forward Flow': A New Measure to Quantify Free Thought and Predict Creativity," *American Psychologist* 74, no. 5 (2019): 539, https://doi.org/10.1037/amp0000391; Cristian Danescu-Niulescu-Mizil et al., "You Had Me at Hello: How Phrasing Affects Memorability," *Proceedings of the ACL*, 2012.

8. Olivier Toubia, Jonah Berger, and Jehoshua Eliashberg, "How Quantifying the Shape of Stories Predicts Their Success," *Proceedings of the National Academy of Sciences of the United States of America* 118, no. 26 (2021): e2011695118, https://doi.org/10.1073/pnas.2011695118.

9. Henrique L. Dos Santos and Jonah Berger, "The Speed of Stories: Semantic Progression and Narrative Success," *Journal of Experimental Psychology: General.* (2022) 151(8):1833-1842 - https://pubmed.ncbi.nlm.nih.gov/35786955/

Chapter 7: What Language Reveals

1. Ryan L. Boyd and James W. Pennebaker, "Did Shakespeare Write *Double Falsehood*? Identifying Individuals by Creating Psychological Signatures with Text Analysis," *Psychological Science* 26, no. 5 (2015): 570–82, https://doi.org/10.1177/0956797614566658.

2. Language use differs by gender (Mehl & Pennebaker 2003; Welch, Perez-Rosas, Kummerfeld, & Mihalcea 2019), for example, age (Pennebaker & Stone 2002; Morgan-Lopez et al., 2017; Sap et al., 2014), race (Preotiuc-Pietro & Ungar, 2018), and political affiliation (Preotiuc-Pietro et al., 2017; Sterling, Jost, & Bonneau, 2020).

3. James W. Pennebaker et al., "When Small Words Foretell Academic Success: The Case

of College Admissions Essays," *PLOS ONE*, December 31, 2014, e115844, https://doi .org/10.1371/journal.pone.0115844; Matthew L. Newman et al., "Lying Words: Predicting Deception from Linguistic Styles," *Personality and Social Psychology Bulletin* 29, no. 5 (2003): 665–75, https://doi.org/10.1177/0146167203251529.

4. The use of language is also associated with a host of health outcomes (see Sinnenberg et al., 2017 for a review), including mental health (de Choudhury, Gamin, Counts, and Horvitz, 2013; Eichstaedt et al., 2018; Guntuku et al., 2017; see Chancellor and De Choudhury 2020 for a review), ADHD (Guntuku et al., 2019), and heart disease (Eichstaedt et al., 2015), often predicting these outcomes better than self-report or SES measures.

5. Sarah Seraj, Kate G. Blackburn, and James W. Pennebaker, "Language Left Behind on Social Media Exposes the Emotional and Cognitive Costs of a Romantic Breakup," *Proceedings of the National Academy of Sciences of the United States of America* 118, no. 7 (2021): e2017154118, https://doi.org/10.1073/pnas.2017154118.

6. Oded Netzer, Alain Lemaire, and Michal Herzenstein, "When Words Sweat: Identifying Signals for Loan Default in the Text of Loan Applications," *Journal of Marketing Research* 56, no. 6 (2019): 960–80, https://doi.org/10.1177/0022243719852959.

7. Reihane Boghrati, "Quantifying 50 Years of Misogyny in Music," Risk Management and Decision Processes Center, April 27, 2021, https://riskcenter.wharton.upenn.edu /lab-notes/quantifying-50-years-of-misogyny-in-music/#:~:text=To percent20look per cent20at percent20misogyny percent20in,is percent20portrayed percent20implicitly percent20in percent20lyrics.

8. Jahna Otterbacher, Jo Bates, and Paul Clough, "Competent Men and Warm Women: Gender Stereotypes and Backlash in Image Search Results," *CHI 17: Proceedings of the 2017 CHI Conference on Human Factors in Computing Systems*, May 2017, 6620–31, https://doi.org/10.1145/3025453.3025727.

9. Janice McCabe et al., "Gender in Twentieth-Century Children's Books: Patterns of Disparity in Titles and Central Characters," *Gender & Society* 25, no. 2 (2011): 197–226, https://doi.org/10.1177/0891243211398358; Mykol C. Hamilton et al., "Gender Stereotyping and Under-representation of Female Characters in 200 Popular Children's Picture Books: A Twenty-First Century Update," *Sex Roles* 55, no. 11 (2006): 757–65, https://doi.org/10.1007/s11199-006-9128-6.

10. Rae Lesser Blumberg, "The Invisible Obstacle to Educational Equality: Gender Bias in Textbooks," *Prospects* 38, no. 3 (2008): 345–61, https://doi.org/10.1007/s11125-009 -9086-1; Betsey Stevenson and Hanna Zlotnik, "Representations of Men and Women in Introductory Economics Textbooks," *AEA Papers and Proceedings* 108 (May 2018): 180–85, https://doi.org/10.1257/pandp.20181102; Lesley Symons, "Only 11 Percent of Top Business School Case Studies Have a Female Protagonist," *Harvard Business Review*, March 9, 2016, https://hbr.org/2016/03/only-11-of-top-business-school-case -studies-have-a-female-protagonist.

11. Nikhil Garg et al., "Word Embeddings Quantify 100 Years of Gender and Ethnic Stereotypes," *Proceedings of the National Academy of Sciences of the United States of America* 115, no. 16 (2018): E3635–44, https://doi.org/10.1073/pnas.1720347115; Anil Ramakrishna et al., "Linguistic analysis of differences in portrayal of movie characters," *Proceedings of the 55th Annual Meeting of the Association for Computational Linguistics* 1 (2017): 1669–78, https://doi.org/10.18653/v1/P17-1153; Liye Fu, Cristian Danescu-Niculescu-Mizil, and Lillian Lee, "Tie-Breaker: Using Language

Models to Quantify Gender Bias in Sports Journalism," July 13, 2016, arXiv, https://doi.org/10.48550/arXiv.1607.03895.

12. "Racial Divide in Attitudes Towards the Police," The Opportunity Agenda, https://www.opportunityagenda.org/explore/resources-publications/new-sensibility/part-iv.

13. Perry Bacon, Jr. "How the Police See Issues of Race and Policing," FiveThirtyEight, https://fivethirtyeight.com/features/how-the-police-see-issues-of-race-and-policing/.

14. Rob Voigt et al., "Language from Police Body Camera Footage Shows Racial Cisparities in Officer Respect," *Proceedings of the National Academy of Sciences of the United States of America* 114, no. 25 (2017): 6521–26, https://doi.org/10.1073/pnas.1702413114.

Epilogue

1. Claudia M. Mueller and Carol S. Dweck, "Praise for Intelligence Can Undermine Children's Motivation and Performance," *Journal of Personality and Social Psychology* 75, no. 1 (1998): 33, https://doi.org/10.1037/0022-3514.75.1.33.

Index

Entries in *italics* refer to charts and illustrations.

About the Author

JONAH BERGER is a marketing professor at the Wharton School of the University of Pennsylvania and the internationally bestselling author of *Contagious, Invisible Influence*, and *The Catalyst*. He's a world-renowned expert on natural language processing, change, social influence, word of mouth, and why products, services, and ideas catch on. Berger has published over seventy papers in top-tier academic journals, and popular accounts of his work often appear in publications like the *New York Times, Wall Street Journal*, and *Harvard Business Review*. He frequently consults for companies like Google, Apple, Nike, and the Gates Foundation, helping them leverage language, drive change, and get their stuff to catch on. He's been named one of Fast Company's most creative people in business and millions of copies of his books are in print in dozens of languages around the world.